THREE STORY METHOD

FOUNDATIONS OF FICTION

J. THORN

ZACH BOHANNON

THREE**STORY**
METHOD

Edited by Eve Paludan

Cover by Yocla Designs

More info at
www.threestorymethod.com
www.thecareerauthor.com

CONTENTS

FOREWORD

I'm embarrassed to admit this.

After all J. Thorn's hard work, I asked him that most annoying question of successful authors. "Hey, how do I do that? What's the sauce? What's the formula?"

We worked together consulting for a few months. All the while, I read his works and Zach Bohannon's books and I wanted to be able to do this kind of thing they could do easily.

Bear in mind that I'm a New York Times bestselling author. Of nonfiction. It's a whole different country.

This book has paths. You can completely sink into any one and find your way to success. Or you can be really smart and read more than one to get a dimensionality to your thinking. Or, and I'm going to say something mean to you: you can read this book and go back to not publishing a novel.

If you read this book and finish it and you DON'T publish a novel, that is all on you and I'm thinking mean things about you. This book covers all the important ground. This is a vital piece of material.

These guys are friends. But they're friends BECAUSE I love their work and trust it. And I can tell you that when I write and publish my fiction novel some time soon, it'll be because I followed the advice in here.

The only people who read forewords are authors. That's something in your favor. Now go earn it by reading this book, and THEN WRITING YOUR OWN DAMNED BOOK ALREADY!

Don't make me grumpy.

Chris Brogan
Boston MA
Go bag ready

PART I

GETTING READY

INTRODUCTION

"How do you turn an idea into a novel?"

It sounds simple enough. You have a great idea. You sit down at the computer. Type. Sell your book to an agent, and ultimately, to a publishing house, or self-publish it. Royalties roll in. But it doesn't work like that. In fact, most brilliant ideas die somewhere between inception and the creation of that blank document titled, "Chapter 1."

When I asked Seth Godin how he decides on which project to begin, he told me, "I don't have a method. I simply know that I must choose. Most people don't embrace that." Pure Seth. Once you've embraced that reality, how do you move forward?

Systems work. Even for creatives. I came to that realization when I started writing in 2009, continuing to develop a system with Zach Bohannon since 2015, because you can't collaborate without a system. A lone artist can sit down at a computer and tell a story in whatever manner she wants, something you can't do when co-writing. But we quickly discovered that our system wasn't just for collaborating. It made our individual writing process more efficient, but more importantly, it made our stories better.

I knew from my days in the classroom that creativity is most vibrant when it has boundaries. We hate deadlines, but the quality of our stories would suffer without them—we know this even though we don't like to admit it.

But those boundaries don't need to be restrictive or formulaic. Three Story Method is a process, not a formula. It's been developed by using the best story methodologies ever created, and you'll hear from some of those creators throughout the book.

Once we started refining our process, we knew others just like us would benefit from it.

I'm excited to share what I've learned with you, but before we get into the methodology, let's cover a few basics about this book and how it was written.

You'll notice that there are two author names on the cover and yet, I'm speaking to you in the first person as J. Thorn.

Zach Bohannon has been my co-writer and business partner for years. We've written and published hundreds of thousands of words together, and our process has remained generally the same—he does the first drafting, and I do the revisions. But we knew right from the beginning that *Three Story Method* would have to be different.

I started my publishing journey in 2009 and have also spent the past 25 years as an educator. I've taught kindergartners how to read and graduate students how to write. Also, I attended an intense training to become a certified

Story Grid editor in 2017 and have been working with clients ever since. I'm a student of Story, having read dozens of books, and consuming countless classes on the craft.

Zach started on his path in 2014, and he came from the corporate side. He doesn't have the same educator experience or training as me, and we concluded (at the same time, although separately) that I needed to be the one to write the first few drafts of this book.

But make no mistake. Three Story Method is *our* process. We've developed it together over the past several years, having published over a dozen novels we've co-written, and it's what we use with our authors in our publishing company, Molten Universe Media.

Rather than trying to write in a plural first person ("we"), the decision was made to write this book in my voice with Zach's help in revisions. I wrote the first draft and then went through several revisions before sharing it with Zach, who helped to refine all aspects of it.

We believe Three Story Method can help all authors, fiction and nonfiction alike. But in case you're reading the sample and trying to decide whether or not this book is for you, it's worth debunking a few common misconceptions.

"But I don't write fiction."

Although the majority of the foundation work of Three Story Method has been done for creating fiction, it works for nonfiction as well. The most effective sales copy and persuasive writing does so through Story and therefore, knowing how to build to a draft will make all of your story-telling better, from sales copy, to email blasts, to narrative nonfiction. Even in the corporate and small business world, modern branding is all about storytelling.

"I don't plot. I'm a discovery writer. I'm a pantser."

We're all plotters. We're all pantsers. This is a false dichotomy that has been the source of many heated debates between writers. As you'll see in the next section, I believe that some level of planning is the best approach, although that doesn't mean you must plot out every single moment of your novel before you begin drafting.

"I don't follow formulas. I'm a creative, an artist."

Another major misconception that exists in the author community is that a process and a formula are the same thing. They are not. A formula is like a recipe. You do this, you get that. A process is a method, a workflow, or a way of doing something. You already have a process even if you think you don't. If you always sit down at a blank page and stare at it until words come into your head, that's a process —not a productive one, but it's a process, nonetheless.

Three Story Method is designed to be flexible, allowing you to go as deep or as shallow as necessary. For example, if you're a discovery writer, you could still write 85% of your novel without beats or an outline. And if you're a plotter, you might only need 50 words to create a story beat for a chapter of 2,000 words, which means that you're "pantsing" 99% of the words written for that chapter.

You can still be creative with Three Story Method because you already have a process. We're here to help you make it better.

"I've read all the books on Story. There's nothing more to learn."

Imagine if Joseph Campbell had believed that? Or Christopher Vogler? Or Kim Hudson? Or Robert McKee? Or Shawn Coyne?

What if Mark Zuckerberg had believed that MySpace was already the established social media of choice?

What if Chipotle had decided that the fast-food marketplace was too saturated for yet another chain?

There have been methodology books before *Three Story Method,* and there will be more that come after. I've read dozens and continue to read them because each author brings something new. I'm a student of Story. I believe that mastering the craft is a lifelong pursuit and anyone who tells you they have it all figured out is not being honest.

To be the best writer you can be, you must constantly be improving, learning. Three Story Method isn't the best or definitive storytelling methodology, but it's one that we've proven works, over and over again.

One quick grammatical note: You'll notice that the word "Story" is capitalized throughout this book because I hold it in such reverence. Story deserves that capital "S" even when it doesn't start a sentence.

WHY YOU NEED THIS BOOK

I can do better.

Every author has had this thought when reading a book. It's not ego and not irrational, but simply human nature—a challenge to our intellect. We talk about the show in a coffee shop after a night at the movies, explaining all the ways the filmmakers got it wrong, no matter how good the movie may have been. Just look at the Amazon 1-star reviews for *Star Wars: A New Hope* and you'll see what I mean.

But *can* you do better? Career authors spend a lifetime trying, never knowing if they'll succeed or not.

We can't do the work for you. We won't reveal the magic hack that will allow you to write and publish a book in 5 days. Our business and lifestyle has been built on honoring systems which develop habits that turn into the result we want. Goals don't work. Systems get things done.

Three Story Method is one such system. We promise that if you apply the techniques, you will see results. You'll come to the blank page with confidence, you'll find your flow on a routine basis, and you'll tell a better story.

The point is that Story is too important not to get right. And if you want to craft stories, you need a plan.

Think of Three Story Method like an architect would a house. You can't build the attic first. Foundations must be laid, and then the floors can be added one at a time, from the ground up.

I didn't create Three Story Method. In fact, it's well over 2,000 years old. In his MasterClass, Aaron Sorkin recommended that all storytellers read Aristotle's *Poetics* because "everything you need to know about Story is in there." He couldn't have been more correct.

As a philosophy minor at the University of Pittsburgh, I had the privilege of attending classes offered by one of the best philosophy departments in the country. This was the early 1990s and we couldn't Google the answers to life's big questions. I spent countless hours reading the works of some of the smartest people who have ever lived and I found myself drawn more to the classics: Socrates, Plato, and of course, Aristotle.

Imagine my surprise when almost 30 years later, I had a reason to visit my old friend, Aristotle. It's worth revisiting a quick summary of *Poetics* because my interpretation of Aristotle's ideas has become the foundation of Three Story Method, even before I took Sorkin's class and realized they were.

Aristotle's ideas have lasted for thousands of years because they are hardwired into us, even if we don't always consciously identify them.

1. "A whole is that which has a beginning, a middle, and an end." This is so obvious as to be genius and yet, so many of us forget that the fundamental structure of ALL Story is three parts.

2. Aristotle identifies the three forms of story which he called, "the medium, the objects, and the manner." A modern interpretation supposes that the intangible elements of Story are comprised of the method in which the story is delivered, the characters and setting within the story's world, and the manner in which the story is presented, which we'll call genre.

3. Every story "must have six parts, which parts determine its quality—namely, Plot, Character, Diction, Thought, Spectacle, Song." We have grouped these six elements into three "stories" and they are the foundations of Three Story Method.

For thousands of years, Aristotle's work, more than any other, has transformed and molded how we create and consume Story. Three Story Method is our way of leveraging his timeless ideas for a modern storyteller, like you.

A note about *Star Wars*

I've decided to use the Lucas classic, *Star Wars: A New Hope,* as a singular example of how Three Story Method could have been used to craft the masterpiece. Of course, I'm reverse engineering the process, but it works. Also, *Star Wars* is universally recognized, and just about every writer I've ever met has seen it. If you haven't, go watch it now. I'll wait.

Now, instead of referencing dozens of movies you've never seen or mentioning many books you've never read, we can work from common ground. One exception to this is that I've decided to use *Star Wars: The Force Awakens* as a way to show how the Virgin's Promise works, compared to the Hero's Journey.

A note about the worksheet

As you move through *Three Story Method*, we will reference the worksheet that is included in the Appendix. You might want to print out a copy and keep it on your desk as you read so that by the time you're finished with the book, you'll also have a rough plan of how to start your next one.

BEFORE WE BEGIN

Before you can revel in the beautiful story you want to share with the world, you've got to *write* it.

Writing sucks.

Writing is the most fulfilling creative endeavor that has ever existed.

If you've had those thoughts in the past week and they came within 5 seconds of each other, this book is for you.

I hate writing. I love having written.

That about sums it up for most of us. I'll do just about anything to avoid coming to the page, which is the single-most enjoyable intellectual experience in my life. It is a paradox of being a creator, dealing with Resistance (capitalized by Steven Pressfield and so I will as well), as Pressfield identified it in *The War of Art*.

When I discovered the *War of Art* in 2012, it reframed my writing career in a way that was empowering. Pressfield defined Resistance as the universal force that keeps us from doing our life's work. It tells us to sleep in, take the day off, or quit because the world already has too many writers. And Resistance never dies, never goes away. In fact, the closer you get to the end of a project, the more powerful Resistance becomes.

Dreaming up an idea for a novel is easy. You've probably done that three times already today. Executing on the idea is another matter entirely. So, once you have the idea, what comes next?

We assemble stories from acts, acts from chapters, chapters from scenes, scenes from paragraphs, paragraphs from beats, beats from words, words from letters. It all starts with those first few letters. It doesn't matter if you're typing the next great American novel on your laptop or dictating a breakthrough nonfiction title destined to change millions of lives, it all starts with arranging letters into sentences, into paragraphs, and so on.

So, why is it so easy, and at the same time, so difficult?

Go to any social gathering, and you'll hear about someone's "book idea." Along with running marathons and finally cleaning out the garage, writing a book is one of those things that many people say they want to do but few ever do. Ideas don't produce great things. Driven people with optimized systems do.

You're special because you've written a book or you're going to write one. This is not a bucket-list item or a pipe dream for you. But it's so easy to fall victim to Resistance, tumbling down into the same pit of forgotten dreams as those people with a great "book idea."

What about your style? What about your unique writer

voice? Award-winning screenwriter and educator Brian McDonald has an interesting take on this in his book, *The Golden Theme*. He wrote, "Young or inexperienced artists are very concerned with style and in recent years, their teachers have been telling them to find their style, their voice. They do not say to them, 'Learn the craft of storytelling.' Instead, they say, 'Find your voice.' This goal of finding one's voice is in direct conflict with the Golden Theme because it is a selfish goal. It comes out of a desire to be noticed...Stories are the collective wisdom of everyone who has ever lived. Your job as a storyteller is not simply to entertain. Nor is it to be noticed for the way you turn a phrase. You have a very important job—one of the most important. Your job is to let people know that everyone shares their feelings—and that these feelings bind us. Your job is a healing art, and like all healers, you have a responsibility. Let people know that they are not alone. You must make people understand that we are all the same."

Clearly, mastering the art of storytelling is important and bigger than you and me.

Now, what do those who have gone before us have to say about the matter?

ADVICE WORTH HEEDING

In one of the most useful and long-lasting books on writing called—wait for it—*On Writing*, Stephen King doles out timeless advice. Don't be fooled by his back catalog or what the haters have said about him. King has quietly become an American institution, creating a style and genre beyond the hack horror novelist at whom critics rolled their eyes in the latter part of the twentieth century. King has become king and any aspiring writer, regardless of platform or genre, is smart to listen to what he has to say.

His biggest piece of advice? Read as much as possible.

Although intellectually it might seem like a no-brainer, you'd be surprised by how many times I hear this phrase from other writers: "I don't have time to read." Ludicrous. As King says, "If you want to be a writer, you must do two things above all others: read a lot and write a lot." You need to be living, eating, and breathing Story. You must internalize story structure that has become part of our collective DNA.

Does it matter what you read? Yes and no. Some might say you should *only* read the kind of story you want to tell because then you'll be able to know the best way to tell your own. That's true.

Some might say you should have a diverse library so that your story is influenced by other elements and your tale will then come together in a way that is uniquely your own. That's true. Bottom line, you need to be reading all the time.

<u>Write the words that are the hardest for you to write.</u>

"The most important things are the hardest things to say," writes King. "They are the things you get ashamed of because words diminish your feelings."

Some in the twenty-first century might call this "therapy," and I, for one, cannot think of a better kind because it doesn't cost me a dime and I don't need a licensed therapist to do it. In short, King believes, "Writing is refined thinking."

Whether you're writing fiction to entertain or nonfiction to inform, writing allows you to work through your own problems and reading your story will help others work through theirs. In other words, take a risk. If there isn't tension and a sense of danger when you're writing, you can't expect the reader to manufacture it.

<u>Write every single day.</u>

Although I don't always follow this piece of advice, I strive to do so. Writing every day keeps the story fresh and present. As King says, "If I don't write every day, the characters begin to stale off in my mind... I begin to lose my hold on the story's plot and pace."

When I first started writing novels in 2008, I had to write

every day before work to keep the story fresh. It took me almost ten months to write a 125,000-word first draft. After a decade of practice and dedication to the craft, I can now write the first draft of a 75,000-word novel in less than two months. Just like anything, the more you do it, the better and more efficient you become.

Many writers set goals, and they believe that will keep them accountable. They say—especially in early January—"I'm going to write more," or, "I'm going to set a word count goal of 1,000 words a day," or, "My goal is to publish a book this year."

The majority of those resolutions are broken by the third week of January, and even fewer of those goals survive the year's first quarter.

I hate goals, and I don't think they work. And when you achieve your goals, you can feel worse than if you had failed.

Let's say you set a goal to lose 20 pounds in 2 months. What if then you go to the gym, change your diet, get plenty of sleep—and when you weigh in after 8 weeks, you've lost 19 pounds? You've failed to reach your goal, and you'll ignore all the progress you've made because you lost 19 pounds instead of 20.

But what if you look down at the scale and realize you've lost 21 pounds? Time for a bowl of ice cream to celebrate, skip the gym on Monday morning, stay up late watching Netflix. Pretty soon, your progress is gone and now, so is your confidence.

Instead, consider developing systems through habit to design the future you want to have. After all, I'm assuming your "goal" isn't to write one book, it's to become a career author—writing and publishing year after year, enough so that you can support yourself and your loved ones by doing what you love.

In James Clear's best-selling book *Atomic Habits*, he illustrates the science around habits and how that, more than anything else, will get you what you want. Clear believes that habits create systems, and that systems will help you design the life you want—not goals.

Writers write. Pure and simple. Take King's advice and write every single day. It won't be easy, and your lizard brain will fight you every step of the way. Resistance will show up the strongest when you're at your weakest. King has famously said that he only takes off two days a year from writing—his birthday and Christmas. If a master of American literature must write every day, you know it's probably best for us mere mortals, too.

Do some simple math, and you'll understand the power in a daily writing habit. If you write 200 words a day for one year, you'll have a draft of 73,000 words, which is the equivalent of a short genre fiction novel.

Certain nonfiction authors write to niche audiences and publish books around 35,000 words, so if you write nonfiction, you'll have two drafts at the end of one year.

Two hundred words. If you can't write 200 words a day, go back to a party and brag about your book idea because you probably don't really want to be an author. The previous four paragraphs total about 200 words.

In her book, *The 8-Minute Writing Habit,* Monica Leonelle suggests that you can build this habit by writing, as the title states, for as little as 8 minutes a day. You might be surprised at how quickly you will surpass that 200-word mark with only 8 focused minutes of writing.

But it's not easy. Nobody ever said it would be.

You're reading this book, which means you've already spiritually committed to getting your book done. Congrats! So where do you begin?

In *Novelist's Boot Camp*, Todd A. Stone lays out the landscape in "Drill 16" which he calls, "Know the Terrain." Stone believes that preparation is the key to success. He suggests you read the books that seem closest to what you want to write, read the recognized masters, read those on the cutting edge, read the bestsellers, and read about the genre.

Notice any patterns in there? All six of the steps in "Know the Terrain" involve reading. If you can't read, you can't write.

Once you've leveled-up your writing game, it's time to chuck the goals and focus on the habits to build your system. That's what this entire book is about.

PANTSER OR PLOTTER?

But before we get into the actionable steps, we must address a long-standing debate among authors: Do you plot or do you pants? Plotting means you sit down and plan what you're going to write. Pantsing (writing by the seat of your pants) means you sit down and "discovery write" or make it up as you go along. Although there is a continuum from unorganized pantsing to a manic plotter, I believe that career authors always employ some level of planning before beginning a project.

As Libbie Hawker states in *Take Off Your Pants!* about the debate between plotting and pantsing, "So at the risk of making myself very unpopular, I'm going to go out on a limb and state boldly that there is, in fact, a superior method for writing a book... IF—and that's a very particular 'if'—your goals include establishing a full-time writing career."

In *Story*, renowned cinematic storytelling guru, Robert McKee writes, "In some literary circles, 'plot' has become a dirty word, tarred with a connotation of hack commercialism... While no fine film was ever written without flashes of fortuitous inspiration, a screenplay is not an accident." He goes on to say that both plot and characterization are critical, and that, "plot is the writer's choice of events and their design in time." In other words, you must have a deliberate plan.

We can probably blame our friend Aristotle for starting the pantsing vs. plotting debate.

In *Classical Storytelling and Contemporary Screenwriting*, Brian Price mentions "Aristotle's dictate" in *Poetics*. As for Story, whether the poet takes it ready-made or constructs it for himself, he should, "First sketch its general outline, and then fill in the episodes and amplify in detail."

The real-world analogies are endless. You can't build a house without a blueprint. You can't plant a garden without determining what seeds you need. Or consider how music is produced. When I would record a song with my band, we didn't start with the vocals or a wailing guitar solo. We had to lay down the foundation for the song. We had to record the drums and bass guitar—the rhythm section—first.

While the analogies make sense for me, there's something even more important that isn't talked about.

Can you write a good story by pantsing? Yes, of course. Eventually. But who wants to spend the time writing thousands of words and then have to throw them out because you wrote yourself into a corner? Who wants to spend three or four times as long revising a draft because you didn't know where you had to take the story? Who wants to hit a wall of Resistance at the end of a draft because you didn't think about how the story would end?

Not me. I know because I've done it. Over the years, I've

watched my fellow writers improve their stories. The ones who have worked hard on their craft, who wanted to reach readers, who wanted to be relevant—they've all moved more toward plotting on the spectrum. All of them.

"I can't plot because I want to be surprised. I want to let the story take me wherever it goes."

This is usually what I hear from less-experienced writers or from writers who have goals instead of dreams. If your "goal" is to write one book, you can do that standing on your head while typing with one hand. It might take you 10 years, but you'll eventually hit your goal if you don't die first. But if you want to write more than one book and make a living as a career author, you simply cannot pants your way there.

Discovery writers must spend significantly more time revising, editing, and paying for help to do both. They waste words, and time, and money. But you knew that already, otherwise, you wouldn't be reading *Three Story Method*, so let's get into it and start setting up a system that will allow you to effortlessly focus on the Story without worrying about waste, inefficiency, or that other name for Resistance —writer's block.

One more common objection I've heard to story methodologies in general is that they're too formulaic and that "my story is unique" and therefore, won't fit into any kind of structure.

In episode 18 of season 3 of "Akimbo," a podcast by Seth Godin, he says, "There are no wholly original thinkers. It is impossible to bring a wholly original thought to the world and have the world do anything at all with it. The best we can hope for is juxtapositions, combinations, a this-and-

that. When we put them together, we have something new...
On a good day, 90-99% of the work I'm doing is about
copying what someone did before me, and then maybe
twisting it a little bit to make it even more useful."

I couldn't agree more.

IMPORTANT WORK

To step back for a moment, it's worth mentioning what's at stake—everything. We live in the age of "fake news" and persuasive half-truths. It is within Story where we find meaning. And even in ancient times, philosophers and politicians knew the power of Story. Plato pleaded with the leaders of Athens to ban poets and storytellers in 388 BC. He believed that storytellers were dangerous because the power of Story could provide us meaning, even if the medium itself was abhorrent.

ON A MORE PERSONAL LEVEL, Story has been how I've made sense of my world. When I was twelve years old, my paternal grandfather died. At the time, I was reading *Pet Semetary* by Stephen King. Although this is definitely a classic of modern horror, it deals with themes surrounding death—like, should we bring back the deceased if we have the power to do so? I remember processing the death of a grandparent by seeing how the characters in King's novel reacted, the decisions they made.

.   .   .

I'M NOT SUGGESTING that a horror novel can replace grief therapy, but fiction can help us make sense of traumatic events. Sadly, but as a testament to the power of Story, my father passed away 35 years after his father, and again, I found myself processing my grief with Story. Only this time, I did it as an author in my own manuscript instead of as a reader.

PART II

THE METHODOLOGY

THREE STORY METHOD OVERVIEW

Three Story Method has been built on Aristotle's timeless method for Story creation, a new interpretation for a modern world.

LIKE BUILDING A HOUSE, a contractor must start with a foundation. Without that, nothing else is possible. Once a strong foundation has been built, other stories are added.

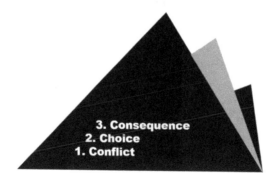

But before we explain how Three Story Method works in threes, let's briefly identify where the "rule of three" appears in the universe.

THE RULE of three is deeply embedded in our very existence and once you begin looking for it, you'll see it everywhere.

OUR OWN MORTALITY is a three-act story: birth, life, death.

IN *IMMEDIATE FICTION*, Jerry Cleaver states, "In its purest form a story is just three elements: conflict, action, resolution. Someone is faced with a problem (conflict) he must struggle with (action), and he wins or loses (resolution)... These story elements are what you will spend your writing life working to master."

MUSIC IS CREATED on the idea of triads. Guitarists know the most satisfying chords to play through a distorted amplifier are those comprised of three notes, also known as "power chords."

IN RELIGION, the idea of the triple Deity is predominant in the Christian faith, but examples span history and culture, including the Buddhist belief in The Three Turnings of the Wheel of Dharma.

. . .

EVEN MOVEMENTS such as Wicca believe in the threefold law, which says that whatever you put into the universe (positive and negative energy) will come back to you threefold.

IN THE NATURAL WORLD, there is almost something mystical about the number three. There are three laws of motion, three types of particles (proton, neutron, electron), three types of electric charges (positive, negative, neutral), and three states of matter (solid, liquid, gas).

THE WAY we conceptualize time is trifold: past, present, and future.

THE HARDY EXPLORERS among us honor the Survival Rule of Three (3 minutes without air, 3 hours without shelter, 3 days without water, 3 weeks without food).

WHEN IT COMES to memory retention, people find it easiest to remember three items and even in modern pop culture, some superstitious folks believe famous people die in patterns of three.

THEREFORE, thousands of years of human existence and language reinforce the idea that the core story elements can be reduced to thirds.

.   .   .

ALTHOUGH ARISTOTLE DEFINED six elements of story in *Poetics*, I found it logical to group those into—you guessed it —thirds.

THE FOUNDATION of this methodology is Plot and Structure, without which nothing else can be built. Once the first story is erected, Genre and Theme sit upon Plot and Structure. Finally, the top story of our pyramid is comprised of Character and World.

Three Story Method: Foundations of Fiction

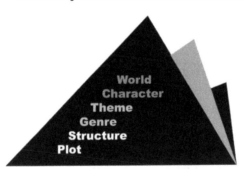

Plot

According to Aristotle, plot is the most important and fundamental part of your Story. I'll show you how to begin crafting yours by using the Pixar Pitch and Blake Snyder's logline.

Structure (Song)

Song is how the plot is structured. My favorite Motown records sound much different than my favorite Metallica records, but both tell a story through song. Song *is* structure. In this section of the book, we'll examine the genesis of Three Story Method in addition to other popular Story methodologies.

Genre (Diction)

Aristotle wrote *Poetics* presumably as a manual for playwrights, but his ideas are applicable across mediums. He even discusses how they fit in Homer's work, including *The Iliad* and *The Odyssey*. For modern audiences, diction has come to mean how you say something. For novelists, this is *genre*. Reader expectations are a language authors must speak, and that language is genre.

Theme (Thought)

The idea of thought can easily be recognized as theme. While it's not always possible to identify theme, Three Story Method provides the tools to answer the question: What's it *really* about?

Character

No ancient Greek translation here. Aristotle placed an importance on the characters and so do I.

. . .

WORLD (Spectacle)

I often think of spectacle as the shows in Las Vegas or the Super Bowl half-time performance, but in terms of Story, it can encompass the idea of the fictional world. Putting "the cherry on top," Three Story Method provides a framework for worldbuilding without the risk of feeding Resistance.

STORY ARCHETYPES

Before getting into the Three Story Method methodology, it's worth revisiting a few of the most popular and well-established story archetypes available to novelists.

If you're familiar with these or want to get straight to preparing your Story, you can skip over this section or reference it later.

Going back to one of the master theorists of Story, Joseph Campbell created and did extensive work in documenting his theory of the Hero's Journey. You've undoubtedly heard of this theory, and you probably recognize some of the terminologies.

A deep dive into Campbell's theory is beyond the scope of this book. However, a quick overview will help put you in the right frame of mind for developing your story's premise —and just as important—its theme.

In 1949, *The Hero with a Thousand Faces* combined Joseph Campbell's expertise in modern psychology and ancient mythology. He demonstrated how the journey's stages can be found almost universally in all of the world's most recognizable myths. Campbell's theory is that the Hero's Journey exists in every culture because it constitutes what it means to be human.

The massive tome is exhaustive but also academic, and while I'd recommend that every writer should read *The Hero with a Thousand Faces* at least once, I know most won't. If you'd like a more condensed and streamlined version, watch *Joseph Campbell and the Power of Myth with Bill Moyers* that aired on PBS in the late 1980s, just a year or so before Campbell died. In it, you can begin to get a sense of his theory and how he developed it. Toward the end of his life, Campbell was said to have had greatly influenced George Lucas with many aspects of the Hero's Journey throughout the original *Star Wars* movies.

With the rise of modern feminism and approaching the new millennium, Maureen Murdock published *The Heroine's Journey* in 1990. Murdock met Joseph Campbell in 1981, and she presented him with her take on the Hero's Journey. She "felt that the focus of female spiritual development was to heal the internal split between a woman and her feminine nature" and she was surprised when he said that women don't need to make the journey.

Campbell told Murdock, "In the whole mythological tradition the woman is *there*. All she has to do is to realize that she's the place that people are trying to get to. When a woman realizes what her wonderful character is, she's not going to get messed up with the notion of being pseudo-male."

Murdock found Campbell's response unsatisfying. In *The Heroine's Journey,* she says, "They do not want to be handmaidens of the dominant male culture, giving service to the gods. They do not want to follow the advice of fundamentalist preachers and return to the home."

And hence, she began her work on identifying the woman's quest, which she believed was, "to fully embrace their feminine nature... It is a very important inner journey toward being a fully integrated, balanced, and whole human being." And as we will see in *The Virgin's Promise*, the idea of an internal journey versus an external one can satisfy both sides of our dualistic nature.

In McDonald's book, *Invisible Ink*, he discusses the need for both feminine and masculine energy in your story.

"The concept of seeing the moon as feminine and the sun as masculine seemed to make sense to me, in an ancient sort of way. And for some reason it stuck with me and I began to look at the two attributes in terms of story. Then I had, what was for me, an epiphany: there are masculine and feminine elements of story. When I put this hypothesis to the test, and applied it to classic stories that have worked over time, it held up. When I then applied it to my own work, it elevated the level of my stories. When I told friends and students, they also found that it helped them...I define masculine elements as external, while feminine elements are internal. Without equal, or close to equal, parts, your story is unbalanced."

A more accessible version of the Hero's Journey was written by Christopher Vogler, *The Writer's Journey: Mythic Structure for Writers*. Vogler worked in Hollywood and taught filmmakers about Story. He's most famous for his consulting role in Disney's *The Lion King,* but he has become known worldwide for his take on Campbell's theory.

He "explores the powerful relationship between mythology and storytelling in his clear, concise style that's made this book required reading for movie executives, screenwriters, playwrights, fiction, and nonfiction writers, scholars, and fans of pop culture all over the world."

Vogler took Campbell's theory and made it more modern and accessible, and it is usually Vogler's adaptation that is widely used today by creatives in many industries. Again, I think *The Writer's Journey* should be required reading for all authors, and although the book's spine is just as thick as *The Hero with a Thousand Faces*, it is a quick read.

To come up with the premise, it's important to at least be able to identify the stages of the Hero's Journey. Without going into great detail, Campbell labels them as: The Call to Adventure, Refusal of the Call, Supernatural Aid, The Crossing of the First Threshold, The Belly of the Whale, The Road of Trials, The Meeting with the Goddess, Woman as the Temptress, Atonement with the Father, Apotheosis, The Ultimate Boon, Refusal of the Return, The Magic Flight, Rescue from Without, The Crossing of the Return Threshold, Master of the Two Worlds, Freedom to Live.

For the Heroine's Journey, Murdock labels the ten stages as Separation from the Feminine, Identification with the Masculine, The Road of Trials, The Illusory Boon of Success, Strong Women Can Say No, The Initiation and Descent to the Goddess, Urgent Yearning to Reconnect with the Feminine, Healing the Mother/Daughter Split, Finding the Inner Man with Heart, Beyond Duality.

And as Vogler is famous for doing, he developed a more streamlined version of Campbell's stages of the Hero's Journey, 12 in all. In *The Writer's Journey,* we have Ordinary

World, Call to Adventure, Refusal of the Call, Meeting with the Mentor, Crossing the First Threshold, Tests Allies Enemies, Approach to the Innermost Cave, Ordeal, Reward (Seizing the Sword) The Road Back, Resurrection, Return with the Elixir. In the book, Vogler includes graphs depicting how the 12 stages spread across the three-act structure.

In addition to the more traditional storytelling methodologies, emerging strategies, such as the use of tarot, Chinese archetypes, or runes, can add another layer of analysis helpful at any stage of the manuscript. Check the Appendix for more information on these.

VOGLER'S 12 STAGES FOR STAR WARS

Here's what Vogler's twelve stages look like for *Star Wars: A New Hope*.

Ordinary World

Luke is a typical teenager, living with his uncle and aunt on the planet Tatooine. He helps them manage the farm and often complains about doing his chores, an ordinary world like any other. But he also shows signs of being discontent when his uncle refuses to let Luke apply to the academy until the following year.

Call to Adventure

"Help me, Obi-Wan Kenobi. You're my only hope." After seeing Princess Leia's hologram projected from a message inside of R2-D2, Luke is enamored with her and the struggle that is happening at the galactic level. He's intrigued and wants to know more and although it's not clear at the time, it will be a call he cannot ultimately refuse.

REFUSAL of the Call

Old Ben, as Obi-Wan is called before he is revealed to be the mentor, suggests to Luke that there might be more to this world than buying droids and helping his Uncle Owen on the farm. But Luke isn't interested yet, tragically believing the situation out there will never ripple back to him on the desolate lands of Tatooine. He has his chores and he's concerned about what will happen if he doesn't attend to them.

MEETING the Mentor

As Old Ben emerges as Obi-Wan Kenobi, a Jedi warrior who fought in the Clone Wars with Luke's father, Luke begins to befriend his real mentor. Obi-Wan saves Luke after an ambush from the Sand People. He offers to teach Luke the ways of the Force, like his father, but Luke again refuses the call. Meeting the Mentor transitions into Crossing the Threshold when Luke returns to the farm to discover his uncle and aunt have been murdered. He says to Obi-Wan, "There's nothing for me here now. I want to learn the ways of the Force and become a Jedi like my father."

CROSSING the Threshold

The threshold for Luke is his journey to the Mos Eisley spaceport where he has now left his old life behind. He is clearly uncomfortable in the Cantina, akin to a country boy walking the big city streets for the first time. Obi-Wan guides and protects Luke, as a good mentor should.

TESTS, Allies, Enemies

Han Solo and Chewbacca join Luke's journey after he hires them to get them off of Tatooine and to the Alderaan System. Stormtroopers try to stop them from leaving, but Luke's new allies help him escape the planet with C-3PO and R2-D2.

APPROACH to the Innermost Cave

On the Millennium Falcon, Obi-Wan Kenobi begins Luke's Jedi training in preparation for the inevitable conflict. They practice lightsaber moves, and Obi teaches him more about the Force. But Alderaan is gone (destroyed by Darth Vader) and in its place is the Death Star, which will represent Luke's innermost cave. He looks at the massive ship and begins to doubt himself and his abilities.

Ordeal

Luke's mentor sacrifices himself, engaging and distracting Darth Vader but ultimately giving up his life so Luke can escape (after Obi-Wan has disabled the Death Star's tractor beam). The ordeal is the obstacle the hero must overcome, which Luke demonstrates by finding and then rescuing Princess Leia.

. . .

Reward (Seizing the Sword)

Luke's sword is the fact that he's now a pilot for the rebels. Ironically, this is exactly what he'd wished for while arguing with his Uncle Owen back in the ordinary world. He will need to wield this weapon to gain the reward of his journey, although against what appears to be insurmountable odds. But Luke is a teenager, full of ambition and a belief that he is invincible. Along with what he's learned about the Force from his mentor, Luke is positioned to fulfill his journey and take the Road Back.

The Road Back

For Luke, his only way back to an ordinary world is to rid this one of the Death Star. And to do so means he must join the other pilots in a suicide mission to attack a known vulnerability of the Death Star, although with a small chance of success. Right before the campaign begins, Han Solo offers to take Luke with him as he's fleeing the Death Star, but Luke refuses because that road doesn't lead back to the ordinary world.

Resurrection

Although Luke doesn't physically die on the mission, he is reborn as a different person. Most of his squadron is shot down, and it appears as though the Empire has successfully fought off the attack until Luke gets a little help from Han Solo, which allows him to make a final attack run in his X-Wing Fighter. Luke's "old self" dies as he pushes the technology aside and taps into the Force as Obi-Wan taught him. He places a perfect shot without his guidance system, destroying the Death Star. Luke is now in the early stages of his resurrection as a Jedi warrior.

RETURN with the Elixir

He doesn't physically return with the magic potion that will change things, but that is represented in the medal ceremony presided over by Princess Leia. Luke doesn't return to Tatooine yet, but he has brought that freedom to others throughout the galaxy, showing that his actions mattered.

HUDSON'S 13 STAGES FOR STAR WARS

Star Wars: A New Hope represents a tight interpretation of Campbell's and Vogler's work. However, the monomyth theory did not adequately describe all stories of growth as we've seen in Murdock's work. And as she refined the theories of Joseph Campbell, so did Kim Hudson with Christopher Vogler's work.

Kim Hudson's book, *The Virgin's Promise*, creates the duality of life experience, the yin to Vogler's (and Campbell's) yang. In fact, Christopher Vogler wrote the foreword for Hudson's book.

Building upon Murdock's work in *The Heroine's Journey*, several themes merge. Murdock says that, "The heroic quest is not about power over, about conquest and domination, it is a quest to bring balance into our lives through the marriage of both feminine and masculine aspects of our nature."

Also, she says, "The task of today's heroine... is to mine the silver and gold within *herself*. She must develop a positive relationship with her inner Man with Heart and find the voice of her Woman of Wisdom to heal her estrangement from the sacred feminine."

A central theme of Hudson's work is the idea that the Virgin's Promise is about an internal journey or enlightenment, rather than an external conquest. She explains that virgin stories are often found in fairy tales, whereas hero stories are myths because fairy tales tend to focus on the aspects of daily life that force retrospection instead of fame and glory on an external journey.

Besides, Hudson doesn't believe in the monomyth. She explains that both the Hero's Journey and the Virgin's Promise comprise both sides of our dualistic nature, and in fact, are complementary and can often be used in the same story.

"The Virgin is driven towards joy, and the Hero is driven away from fear. Together they represent two fundamental drives in human nature." The energies can be masculine or feminine, meaning stories involving a male protagonist can follow a Virgin's Promise archetype.

Like Coyne does in *Story Grid*, Hudson cautions against using the Virgin's Promise as a template or recipe. She says, "...repeated use of the same representations results in stereotypes and the loss of archetypal power."

Hudson calls her stages "beats," identifying 13 of them.

Dependent World

The virgin begins here, conforming to the societal expectations while denying her true nature.

Price of Conformity

Because she cannot be herself, the virgin pays the price, which takes a toll and creates a "poverty of personal expression."

Opportunity to Shine

But she is then given a chance to explore her potential, an inciting incident of sorts that reveals her dream or talent.

Dresses the Part

This is the moment where the virgin is happy, fulfilled, and when she believes a joyous and meaningful life is possible.

Secret World

Because she is not yet ready to share her gift in the Dependent World, the virgin creates a secret world where she can continue to explore it.

No Longer Fits Her World

The longer she spends in the Dependent World and the Secret World, the more she realizes that she cannot coexist in both and becomes increasingly disenchanted with the Dependent World.

Caught Shining

When it becomes apparent that the two worlds cannot be kept apart, the virgin is caught shining, which leads to a punishment or banishment of some kind.

Gives Up What Kept Her Stuck

This moment is the turning point of the archetypical

journey where the virgin must sacrifice something from her old life in order to potentially create a new one.

Kingdom in Chaos

As the virgin begins to change, it affects the stability of the Dependent World, often manifested in chaos as the structure of society begins to come apart.

Wanders in the Wilderness

She realizes she no longer has the Dependent World as a fail-safe and therefore, the virgin must wander the wilderness in order to follow her dream.

Chooses Her Light

Finally, the virgin believes enough of herself to pursue that dream or passion and this is the last stage of her personal transformation.

Re-Ordering (Rescue)

Coming out of chaos, the kingdom now reforms where it recognizes the virgin's true value and brings her back into the community.

The Kingdom is Brighter

Because of the virgin's pursuit of her authentic dream, the kingdom now realizes how much better things are and how much change had been needed, thanks to her.

I was so intrigued by *The Virgin's Promise* that I posed a few questions to Kim Hudson. Excerpts from that interview which took place in March 2019 can be found in the Appendix.

The Virgin's Promise – *Star Wars: The Force Awakens*

Here's what Hudson's thirteen beats look like for *Star Wars: The Force Awakens*. Notice that unlike the Hero's Journey, the Virgin's Promise is nonlinear so the beats can occur in any order.

Dependent World

Rey is tied to her dependent world. We see this literally in her first scene when she's suspended by a cable that has her tethered to her home planet of Jakku. She is a metal scrapper, barely surviving on what she finds and her life is dependent on the food portions she's accepted in a trade for her scrap.

Price of Conformity

Her "poverty of personal expression" is symbolized in her poverty as a metal scrapper. We see that she follows the rules, stands in line, does what she's supposed to do and for that, she pays the price. Rey is disrespected and exploited by the ruling class represented by Unkar Plutt.

Opportunity to Shine

Rey's potential "ticket out" is when Unkar Plutt offers her 60 portions for the BB-8 droid, a small fortune in that dependent world. She realizes the value of that droid without knowing why. Stepping out of line becomes her inciting incident, a moment when she deviates from societal expectations.

Dresses the Part

When Unkar Plutt sends a few goons to rough up Rey and steal the droid, she "dresses the part" of a tough metal scrapper. She defends BB-8 and fights off the goons, believing that she is protecting her livelihood and future, as any scrapper would. Although not happy, she does seem to be fulfilled at the moment by her victory over the thieves.

Secret World

Rey leaves Jakku for the first time aboard the Millennium Falcon, transitioning from the dependent world to her secret world. She is shown the projected map from BB-8, and she realizes that there is much of the "secret world" to explore, including what Han Solo tells her about the Force. "It's the truth," he says. "All of it."

No Longer Fits Her World

Realizing that she no longer belongs on Jakku and in her dependent world, Rey lands on D'Qar where she sees more "green" than she thought existed in the entire galaxy. When Han Solo offers her a blaster and a job on his ship, she turns him down. Rey realizes that she can't exist in both worlds and says that she must get home to Jakku, even though she has become disenchanted with that life.

Caught Shining

Luke's lightsaber has been left on D'Qar. When Rey finds it, she has a vision where she realizes her true potential. When Maz finds Rey, she tells the girl, "The person you're waiting for is not coming back." With this news, Rey is being punished for shining and again says that she must return home to Jakku.

Kingdom in Chaos

The First Order, looking for Rey and the BB-8 droid, begin destroying planets, which put the "kingdom" in disarray. The ships eventually land on Takodana where Maz and her outlaws live, the ones who have been protecting and hiding Rey. The First Order attacks and chaos reigns.

Wanders in the Wilderness

Rey literally runs through the wilderness of Takodana as she's fleeing from Kylo Ren. She cannot return to Jakku and therefore, she must flee toward a new and uncertain future.

Gives Up What Kept Her Stuck

In the turning point of her archetypical journey, Rey sacrifices her own safety by resisting Kylo Ren's mental manipulation, but he is still able to read some things in her mind. She knows that her old ways and life are now gone and that she is in the process of creating a new one.

Chooses Her Light

Now, Rey believes she can pursue her dream. In the final fight with Kylo Ren, she uses the Force to summon the lightsaber. Also, she fends off his mental manipulation again as she refuses his offer to teach her the dark side of the Force. She has chosen her light, and to fight on the side of light for the Resistance. The first hint of Rey's choice comes a few scenes earlier when she uses the Force to convince a stormtrooper to let her go, in much the same way that Obi-Wan Kenobi did in *Star Wars: A New Hope*.

Re-Ordering (Rescue)

She lands back on D'Qar where Princess Leia greets Rey with a hug, recognizing her true value and welcoming her back into the community.

The Kingdom is Brighter

When Princess Leia tells Rey, "May the Force be with you,"

she is acknowledging that the "kingdom is brighter" because of Rey. Also, Rey pilots the Millennium Falcon to the remote planet where Luke Skywalker has been living and delivers his lightsaber to him, another "bright" moment for Rey and the kingdom.

HERO'S JOURNEY VS. VIRGIN'S PROMISE

Although the Hero's Journey is linear and the Virgin's Promise is not, Hudson compared the two within the typical three-act structure.

Hero's Journey (Vogler)	Virgin's Promise (Hudson)
Act 1	Act 1
Ordinary World	Dependent World
Call to Adventure	Price of Conformity
Refusal of the Call	Opportunity to Shine
Meeting with the Mentor	Dresses the Part
Crossing the First Threshold	
Act 2	Act 2
Tests, Allies, Enemies	Secret World
Approach to the Innermost Cave	No Longer Fits Her World
The Ordeal	Caught Shining
Reward	Gives Up What Kept Her Stuck
	Kingdom in Chaos
Act 3	Act 3
The Road Back	Wanders in the Wilderness
The Resurrection	Chooses Her Light
Return with the Elixir	Re-Ordering (Rescue)
	The Kingdom is Brighter

PLOT

Why Plot is First

Plot is not only the cornerstone and foundation of your Story, but it is also the frame. Plot extends up from the bottom and is what other elements of story (such as theme and character) hang on.

WITHOUT PLOT, you have characters engaging in interesting ways, but no Story.

ALTHOUGH I DON'T BELIEVE that plot and character are at odds, Aristotle put his flag into plot.

"THE PLOT, then, is the first principle, and, as it were, the soul of a tragedy: Character holds the second place."

· · ·

CHARACTER IS vital and absolutely necessary, but character is revealed by plot.

How DO you lay the cornerstone of your plot foundation?

A STORY IDEA IS BORN

It happens in the strangest of places. You're walking the dog or taking the trash can to the curb when inspiration strikes. Story idea! But you're an author, so you file it away with the other 400 ideas you had while standing in the shower that morning.

WE KNOW that when someone at a party offers us their "brilliant" idea for a novel, we politely listen and nod with the understanding that ideas are cheap. We all have a million of them. The *execution* of the idea is almost impossible, which is why 99% of those brilliant ideas will never become stories.

BUT THAT IDEA *you* had won't go away easily. It fidgets its way into your brain while you're cooking dinner. It reappears in the bottom of the dirty laundry basket. It shows up at your child's oboe recital. You know that if you don't deal with this beast, it'll soon consume you.

· · ·

THE IDEA for a postapocalyptic novel came to me one chilly, autumn morning. I live in Cleveland, Ohio, and folks at that time of the year begin to pack up their boats and store the summer furniture and toys. I remember walking through the leaves and savoring the smells of fall when an idea came to me: What if you could avoid an apocalyptic event by living on a boat on Lake Erie? And what would happen when the great lake froze in the winter? These questions that came out of a simple stroll gave me the inspiration for what would become the *BARREN* trilogy.

ZACH HAD an idea come to him while walking down the hallway at his former job and seeing one of his employees spending his lunch break by taking a nap inside an unoccupied office. He asked himself, "What if he woke up and everyone in the building had turned to zombies?" This simple thought led to his *Empty Bodies* series, which he self-published and earned him enough royalties to quit said job and become a career author.

BUT HOW DO you know if it's worth your time to pursue your idea? The first litmus test is to put it through a filter created by Stephen King—an ordinary person in an extraordinary situation.

FROM IMDB.COM

"Luke Skywalker joins forces with a Jedi Knight, a cocky pilot, a Wookiee and two droids to save the galaxy from the Empire's world-destroying battle station, while also attempting to rescue Princess Leia from the mysterious Darth Vader."

LUKE, the ordinary kid, thrown into an extraordinary, intergalactic rebellion.

THERE ARE HUNDREDS, thousands of stories with this underlying premise. Character is king, regardless of genre, including nonfiction. Whether you're writing the tales of Zinzu on the planet Fardicon or chronicling how you conquered your fear of snakes—on planes—every story is about a person, a character. I don't believe in the dichotomy of plot-driven versus character-driven storytelling. Every good story must have a magnetic protagonist *and* an engaging plot. You need both.

IN *CREATING CHARACTER ARCS*, K.M. Weiland also says that you need both. "Plot and character are integral to one another. Remove either one from the equation (or even just try to approach them as if they were independent of one another), and you risk creating a story that may have awesome parts, but which will not be an awesome whole."

NEIL GAIMAN, in a session on MasterClass.com, says that authors should use memorable lies to communicate truth and that all fiction must be honest and specific. It might seem like a paradox but getting specific and memorable is great advice.

· · ·

IN *STORY*, McKee writes, "We cannot ask which is more important, structure or character, because structure *is* character; character *is* structure. They're the same thing, and therefore one cannot be more important than the other." Therefore, Three Story Method emphasizes the focus on structure *and* character.

TIME TO LET your killer idea out of its cage. Does it involve an ordinary person in an extraordinary situation? If not, can you tweak it so that it does? The key here is that "ordinary" and "extraordinary" are relative terms. If you want to tell a story about a psychic ninja, battling the Japanese mob might be the "ordinary" so what pulls this supernatural warrior out of *his* normal life? What is extraordinary for *him*?

STORIES ARE CHANGE. Period. If nothing changes, there is no conflict, and thus, you have no story. Instead, you have what I like to call a lukewarm series of somewhat interesting events. That's fine for water cooler chatter at the office or a dinner conversation at the family holiday gathering, but it is not a novel.

WEILAND IDENTIFIES SEVERAL ARCS, the Positive Change Arc being the most common. "Plot, in its simplest manifestation, is all about the protagonist's thwarted goal... The Positive Change Arc, in its simplest manifestation, is all about the protagonist's changing priorities. He realizes the reason he's not getting what he wants in the plot is because either: a) He wants the wrong thing. b) His moral methods for achieving what he wants are all wrong."

TAKE that killer idea and re-frame it through the ordinary and extraordinary situation of the main character. If your idea involves a setting or a situation, now is the time to create a character and put her into it. If there is no extraordinary element in your killer idea, it's not killer.

BUT THEN THINGS get complicated because a killer idea that includes a protagonist in an extraordinary situation is only a start. Yes, you're the author and also the first reader. But hopefully, you're not the only reader. At some point, regardless of how you decide to share your story with the world, you *will* have to share it with the world. Because you're a storyteller.

PEOPLE ARE (or seem to be) busier than ever before. And, our entertainment and informational choices have exploded since the rise of the Internet. If your eventual goal is to publish your work, it's important to remember that your book isn't competing with other books. That attention is being vied for by social media, Netflix, games, podcasts, and more. Now, more than any other time in the history of publishing, you need to know the genre conventions and reader expectations, or nobody will read your book.

THEREFORE, you must start building your Story's foundation with a succinct and simple premise—The Pixar Pitch.

THE PIXAR PITCH

Presenting an idea to someone else or to yourself is incredibly important. In my days of teaching entrepreneurship to high school students, the pitch process forced students to refine and focus an idea into something easily explained. And if you can't easily explain the idea, it's too complicated, and you need to take a step back and rethink it.

In the entrepreneurial world, it's called an "elevator pitch," and the name comes from the idea that if you had a potential investor trapped in an elevator, how would you close the deal in a matter of seconds?

While you probably shouldn't be stalking potential readers in elevators, there is a way to "pitch" your idea without getting arrested or getting slapped with a restraining order. And luckily for you, one of the greatest storytelling factories in the world created a template for you: The Pixar Pitch.

Brian McDonald used a slightly modified version of the Pixar Pitch in his book, *Invisible Ink*.

In *To Sell is Human*, Daniel Pink discusses the effectiveness of using a method created by movie executives at Pixar Studios. These folks are responsible for listening to and vetting the ideas that will eventually head into production with budgets of millions of dollars, meaning there's a lot at stake—and it all starts with the idea. The *pitch*.

The Pixar Pitch is the first section on the worksheet under the title "Plot." The Pixar Pitch formula is simple on the surface. But it's deceptive as once you try creating one, you'll realize how difficult it is to come up with a killer story idea.

Once upon a time_____. Every day, _____. One day _____. Because of that, _____. Because of that, _____. Until finally, _____.

Here's a reverse-engineered version of *Star Wars: A New Hope*:

Once upon a time, there lived a boy named Luke. Every day, he helped his uncle on the farm and with the droids. One day he stumbles upon a mysterious message from Princess Leia. Because of that, he meets Obi-Wan, who explains his Jedi heritage. Because of that, he is drafted into the Rebellion's air fleet. Until finally, he lands the perfect shot to destroy the Death Star.

Our buddy Aristotle may have pre-dated Pixar. Here's what he said about Homer's *Odyssey* in *Poetics*:

"Thus the story of the Odyssey can be stated briefly. A certain man is absent from home for many years; he is jealously watched by Poseidon, and left desolate. Meanwhile his home is in a wretched plight—suitors are wasting his substance and plotting against his son. At length, tempest-tost, he himself arrives; he makes certain persons acquainted with him; he attacks the suitors with his own hand, and is himself preserved while he destroys them."

That's it. Take your ordinary character and extraordinary situation and run it through the Pixar Pitch template. Create three versions and see which one you like best or the one that others like best. It'll take several drafts of each, for sure. Keep tweaking them until you're so intrigued by your own ingenuity that you can see the royalty checks rolling in. Take a deep breath and come back to reality. Now it's time to test your pitches.

Take your pitches to your audience or fans of the genre. Don't share them with your spouse, kids, significant other, neighbors, family, or friends *unless* they're a huge fan of the genre. And even if they are, take it with a grain of salt. They know you. You have a relationship. They'll try to please you or anger you, depending on the nature of your relationship. Either way, the opinion of family and friends in any aspect of your author career is fraught with bias so avoid it.

Post on social media, try your pitches on strangers in a coffee shop, take them to a critique group. And forget about the fear that someone is going to steal your killer idea. Remember, there's no such thing as a unique story, which means someone has most likely already told yours.

And remember that an idea does not make a novel. Two writers could take the same Pixar Pitch and end up with radically different novels. The fear of having your intellectual property stolen is unfounded, especially this early in the process. And even once the book is published, obscurity is a far worse consequence than piracy.

Let's assume you have a clear pitch winner (keep going until one emerges)—people love it. You've crafted a hooky Pixar Pitch and then revised it after soliciting feedback from the people who don't know you well or don't have a relationship with you.

Now you're ready to turn the Pixar Pitch into a logline.

THE LOGLINE

In *Save the Cat!*, Blake Snyder raises the ultimate question for screenwriters and novelists alike.

"But what's it about?"

Blake writes, "I talk to lots of screenwriters, I've been pitched by experts and amateurs, and my question when they prematurely drift into the story of their movie is always the same: 'What's the one-line?' Oddly, this is often the last thing screenwriters think about when writing a script... [if] You can't get to the heart of the story in less than 10 minutes. Boy are you screwed."

The logline or one-line has four components: irony, a compelling mental picture, audience and cost, and a killer title.

Irony is used as the hook. For example, here's Blake's logline for *Pretty Woman*: A businessman falls in love with a hooker he hires to be his date for the weekend. The irony *is* the hook.

The compelling mental picture must show potential for an entire story. Another Snyder example is the logline for *Die Hard*: A cop comes to L.A. to visit his estranged wife, and her office building is taken over by terrorists. In this one-line, we can see an entire movie unfolding in this hostage situation.

Here's one I wrote for *Star Wars: A New Hope*: A teenage boy from a remote planet discovers a mysterious power that he must trust to defeat a galactic, evil empire.

The logline is effective because it forces you to narrow your story to the core, to what matters. Notice there's no mention of lightsabers or Wookiees, or whether Greedo shot first. Those are interesting worldbuilding elements that help make *Star Wars* a unique intellectual property, but they're not what the story is about. When developing your plot, your priority is trimming your story concept down to the most basic element.

What Snyder describes as audience and cost can be extrapolated to book genre. Again, you must know who this story is for and what conventions you must deliver. More on that in the section on Genre.

Although I don't believe the title is as important at this stage of the creative process, it can help pull together the concept and the audience. Our favorite books, movies, television shows, and video games conform to certain consumer expectations.

A viewing of *The Walking Dead* is delivering a far different experience than *Downton Abbey,* and the experience is embedded in the title. These are two excellent examples of brilliant titles.

According to Snyder, the most important aspect of the title

is that "It says what it is." Forget being cute or clever and tell the reader exactly what she can expect.

The Walking Dead is about the walking dead. The title is straightforward and yet nuanced. If you've never watched the show, it features zombies. Lots of them. But it also chronicles the life of the survivors and at different points in the show, "the walking dead" title could apply to the humans as much as the undead.

"Along with a good 'What is it?' a movie must have a clear sense of what it's about and who it's for. Its tone, potential, the dilemma of its characters, and the type of characters they are, should be easy to understand and compelling." Everything that Snyder wrote about screenwriting in *Save the Cat!* applies to novels as well.

Before you put pen to paper or rest your hands on the keyboard, you *must* go through this process to vet and improve your idea. No amount of developmental edits, peer critiques, or author coaching sessions can rescue a lame premise. If your idea isn't engaging, simple, tight, and intriguing, everything else you do will be a complete waste of time.

Go to the worksheet and create a logline in the "Plot" section beneath the Pixar Pitch drafts you wrote.

STRUCTURE

THE PYRAMID

As we've seen, the power of three is a phenomenon we can observe in all aspects of life.

ARISTOTLE RECOGNIZED the power of three and understood it to be a foundational concept within the universe. In *Poetics,* he describes three elements of Story: Suffering, Reversal of the Situation, and Recognition.

MY CONTEMPORARY INTERPRETATION for Three Story Method is Conflict, Choice, and Consequence. Let's take a closer look at each component of the Three Story Method pyramid.

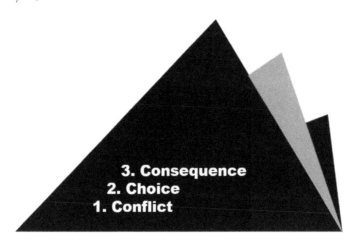

Conflict

The thing that yanks your protagonist out of his ordinary life. Yes, it's that simple. The term "Inciting Incident" is often used in screenwriting and movie production as well as novel writing, but we chose to call it "conflict" because it's more specific. This single event does not necessarily need to be tense, dramatic, or a life-or-death situation—the nature of the inciting incident will depend on your genre. However, it does need to force the main character into changing, which then "incites" the story. Without change precipitated by conflict, there is no story.

IN *THE GOLDEN THEME*, McDonald wrote, "Compelling stories contain conflict because conflict is always about the struggle to survive. You may think that interpersonal conflicts are not about survival because they are not about being eaten, but understanding how to get along with others can be a useful survival skill."

FURTHERMORE, conflict is essential because, as McDonald goes on to explain, conflict threatens our survival and "...survival information is, I believe, the reason we tell stories. We are engaged by stories that contain this kind of information. Not only that, but we also feel compelled to spread this information by repeating the story to others...A strong story that contains solid survival information can survive for thousands of years...Stories are a way to get the benefit of someone else's experience without having to have the experience oneself."

USING MALCOLM GLADWELL'S "10,000-HOUR RULE," we can borrow the experience of others without having to spend all 10,000 hours on our own, which is another way of explaining why survival information is so critical to us and has been for thousands of years.

THROUGHOUT THIS SECTION, I'll provide examples of the pyramid by labeling where they occur in *Star Wars: A New Hope*. Once you begin to internalize and observe the rule at work, you'll never look at Story the same way!

AT ABOUT THE 21-minute mark of the movie, Luke stumbles upon the message Princess Leia had hidden in R2-D2, "Help me, Obi-Wan Kenobi, you're my only hope." This moment of conflict "incites" the story because Luke's world is upended. His curiosity gets the better of him, and he cannot go back to the way things were before he found the droid with the hidden video message.

THIS IS the age of Story, and the best stories have the Conflict, Choice, and Consequence embedded in them. Why fight thousands of years of storytelling evolution?

CHOICE

"The choice between good and evil or between right and wrong is no choice at all." – Robert McKee

IN EVERY UNIT OF STORY, your protagonist must face a choice. I need to repeat this: *There must be a choice.* In all of my client work over the years, this is the single-most challenging concept for most authors to conceptualize.

THE CHOICE IS a difficult decision the protagonist must face, born from a challenging question with equally wonderful or horrific consequences. The best Choice in any story leaves the reader (1) arguing with himself over which option is best for the character and (2) unable to put the book down, insistent on finding out what the character decides.

IF A MAN MUST CHOOSE between killing an intruder in his bedroom in the middle of the night or allowing the intruder to harm his family, this might be intense, but it is not a Choice because the decision is not a difficult one.

HOWEVER, if the intruder has the man's wife and is using her as a human shield, then the man must decide whether or not to fire his gun. If he does, he could kill the intruder and protect his family, but he could also accidentally shoot or hurt his wife. If he doesn't, he won't be risking his wife's life, but the intruder could harm her or the family anyway. *That* is a Choice because the options are equally challenging. People could make legitimate arguments for either course of action, and some people might make one decision in one circumstance but not in another.

DETERMINING the intensity of the Choice is often a case of splitting hairs and not nearly as important as making sure the question facing the main character is a supremely *difficult* one. We are compelled to turn the page or keep watching when we empathize with the character, running the odds on the consequence of the decision as if it were our own. Make it difficult on the character and your reader will follow.

ABOUT 115 MINUTES into *Star Wars*, our hero faces his most serious decision of the story: Does Luke rely on his computer to make the shot, but knowing he's going too fast, and a more experienced pilot has already missed, and Luke is their last chance or does Luke turn off the computer and use the Force that he hasn't mastered and others look at cynically?

. . .

CONSEQUENCE

On the nature of consequence, Aristotle says, "Actions capable of this effect must happen between persons who are either friends or enemies or indifferent to one another. If an enemy kills an enemy, there is nothing to excite pity either in the act or the intention—except so far as the suffering in itself is pitiful. So again with indifferent persons. But when the tragic incident occurs between those who are near or dear to one another—if, for example, a brother kills, or intends to kill, a brother, a son his father, a mother her son, a son his mother, or any other deed of the kind is done— these are the situations to be looked for by the poet."

IN OTHER WORDS, high-stakes consequences arise when the choice facing the character is incredibly difficult, such as a brother contemplating the murder of a family member. The more difficult the choice, the more engaged the reader will be.

WHILE SOCRATES BELIEVED that knowing what is right will result in people doing it, Aristotle disagreed with this nature of knowledge. Aristotle understood that sometimes people fail to do "the right thing" even when they know it's wrong. These philosophical ideas are useful in thinking through the choices you present your characters and the subsequent consequences they face.

. . .

THE CONSEQUENCE IS the answer to the Choice as well as the new circumstance resulting from it.

AT 117 MINUTES, Luke turns off his computer-aided navigation system to use the Force to take the shot at the Death Star's single vulnerability, successfully blowing it up and saving the day.

THE RESULTING circumstance for this decision often creates, "the new normal," the action that resets the life of the protagonist. She's had her life upended, gone through a series of ordeals, been forced to make a difficult decision, and then suffered the consequence of that decision. So, what now?

THE CONSEQUENCE ANSWERS THAT QUESTION, and it can also set the stage for the next Conflict at the scene, chapter, or act level.

IN THE TRIUMPHANT final scene of *Star Wars,* and a minute after Luke makes his decision, his "new normal" is that he has been honored as an intergalactic hero as he's awarded a medal by Princess Leia, completing his "hero's journey" in this installment of the series.

3 ACTS OR 4 ACTS?

The first step in creating the 12 Stages is developing three acts. As Aristotle has proven, all Story breaks down to a beginning, a middle, and an end. It's impossible to have a story that is missing one of those three basic components. In *Story Grid*, Coyne calls these the Beginning Hook, Middle Build, and Ending Payoff. In Three Story Method, we're calling these acts and will stick with the three-act structure.

GENERALLY SPEAKING, the first and third acts comprise 25% of the story while the second act comprises 50% of the story so that you have a 25/50/25 ratio. Like many aspects of story-telling, this is not a strict rule, but straying too far can disorient readers because many stories do conform to this structure.

SOME METHODOLOGIES UTILIZE the four-act structure, and you'll often see these used by screenwriters and movie producers. But you know I like to keep things as simple as possible and not overcomplicate matters. You could plan a story using a four-act or five-act or six-act structure, but it's not necessary.

IN FACT, I believe many storytellers use the four-act structure as a crutch because it's difficult to keep the narrative drive and readers' attention through what has been affectionately nicknamed, "the soggy middle." Half of the book is the second act, which means the story must "spiral up" to the Conflict scene of the third act where the story's momentum will carry the reader through.

BUT IT'S hard to do that and why I believe the four-act structure emerged, allowing the author to hit a Choice and Consequence in the middle of the second act before resetting and doing it again in the third act while having to cover only half as much story real estate. In fact, I believe that many authors turn to the four-act structure because they aren't properly building up to their second act Choice through difficult obstacles, or even because their Choice isn't strong enough. Basically, I see the four-act structure as a cheat.

Three Story Method: Three Act Structure

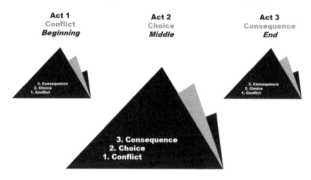

Go to the worksheet and fill out the boxes in the "Structure" section, using *Star Wars* as an example. These will change and evolve as you go through the process so the goal is to get down something workable, not something perfect.

12 STAGES

Now that you have a Pyramid for each Act, you'll need to create a Pyramid for each key scene—the 12 Stages of your entire story.

Three Story Method: 12 Stages

Act 1

Conflict   Choice   Consequence

Act 2

Conflict   Obstacle   Obstacle   Obstacle   Choice   Consequence

Act 3

Conflict   Choice   Consequence

The Pyramids for each act tend to be easier to create because they must be major events in the story. But sometimes I struggle while developing the 12 Stages. It's easy to go with the first idea that pops into your head... but beware, those are rarely the best ideas.

How do you know if the 12 Stages are "good enough?" You can go with what comes first, and that will feel natural to you as the writer, but those scenarios are probably not as interesting to the reader who has seen them often. Or, you can go beyond what's expected, which will force you as the author to spend more time and mental calories, but in the end, you'll surprise and entertain the reader.

The paradox here is that you want to come up with something that is what the reader expects—but different. Genre is the answer which we'll discuss next. If you know the genre well, you'll already know which conventions and tropes you must honor and which ones you can try to innovate.

For example, I primarily write postapocalyptic and dystopian fiction, which are subgenres of science fiction. Readers of postapocalyptic stories expect a "lone cowboy" protagonist who is trying to keep himself alive. This is a convention of the genre. If I wrote a postapocalyptic story without a lone cowboy protagonist, the reader might put the book down. Or say something like, "I wasn't into it." Or, "It didn't hold my attention." Or, "The story didn't grab me." All of those examples are reader code for, "You didn't honor the genre convention that I think is important."

But on the other hand, if you create a lone cowboy protagonist that looks, talks, and acts like Will Smith in *I Am Legend*, readers will say you're "ripping off" the movie or that it's "not original," or "boring." It might seem like a Catch-22. How do you make something alike but different?

Go with your fourth or fifth idea. As you begin to think about what happens to your protagonist in each of the 12 Stages, your instinct will be to jot down the first idea that pops into your head. The story might come clean and fast, and you might get excited.

But there's a problem. Those ideas are coming fast because you've probably seen or read them dozens of times in your life. You're simply grabbing what's on the top of your mind as it pertains to the story and those ideas are probably a composite of dozens or hundreds of other stories that used those elements.

They're not wrong, they're just not interesting. If you go too far in the other direction, you might come up with completely "original" ideas for the 12 Stages, but they'll be too far beyond what that genre reader expects, and now, you're not delivering the story you promised when you identified your genre.

A NEW HOPE EXAMPLE WITH THE 12 STAGES

Let's take a look at the 12 Stages for *Star Wars: A New Hope*.

Act i

Conflict

Luke buys the droids (R2-D2 and C-3PO) from the Jawa traders, even though he probably shouldn't. This simple decision kicks off the first act.

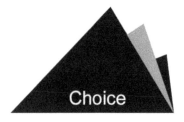

CHOICE

Does Luke accept Kenobi's invitation to train as a Jedi so he can honor his father and join the rebellion or does Luke, being obedient and dutiful, deny the invitation and go back to his uncle's farm?

CONSEQUENCE

Luke turns down the invitation, taking what he believes is the more practical and logical approach. At this point, he doesn't believe that some random kid can have an impact in the world. He begrudgingly accepts that perceived reality.

.   .   .

Act 2

Conflict

Ben and Luke return to the farm where they discover that stormtroopers have killed Luke's uncle and aunt, and then burned the house and farm to the ground.

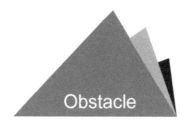

Obstacle

Luke and his small band must board the Death Star to rescue Princess Leia. In the second act, this complicates the situation for Luke and also marks a turn as he becomes openly rebellious.

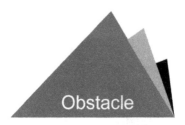

OBSTACLE

The Millennium Falcon is captured and they must hide in Han Solo's smuggling compartments.

OBSTACLE

Luke, Leia, Chewbacca, and Solo become trapped in an infested garbage compactor that threatens to crush them all.

*NOTE - OBSTACLES DO NOT ALWAYS HAVE to occur within the

second act. They are placed here to demonstrate the conventional 25/50/25 length of the three-act structure.

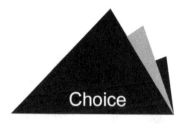

CHOICE

Does Luke interfere with the lightsaber duel between Obi-Wan Kenobi and Darth Vader, saving his mentor but risking his life, or does he sacrifice Kenobi on behalf of the rebellion and get Princess Leia out of harm's way?

CONSEQUENCE

He decides to save the princess while watching Darth Vader strike down Kenobi.

. . .

ACT 3

Conflict

With Han Solo at the helm of the Millennium Falcon, Luke and the others escape the Death Star, thanks to Kenobi's sacrifice, as he had disabled the tractor beam that would have kept the ship in the dock.

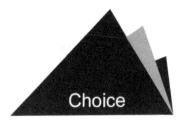

CHOICE

Does Luke rely on his computer to make the shot, but

knowing he's going too fast and a more experienced pilot has already missed and Luke is the last chance, or does Luke turn off the computer and use the Force that he hasn't yet mastered and others look at cynically?

CONSEQUENCE

Luke turns off his computer-aided navigation system to use the Force to take the shot at the Death Star's single vulnerability, successfully blowing it up and saving the day. The "happy ending" occurs when Luke discovers his "new normal." He has transformed from whiny farm boy to intergalactic hero as he's awarded a medal by Princess Leia.

DRAFTING YOUR 12 STAGES

The best approach is to brainstorm a running list for each of your 12 Stages. Write the first idea for all of them—but don't stop there. Keep asking yourself, "What if?" Dig down and come up with a second, third, and fourth variation on your original scene idea, each time trying to put an interesting twist or spin on it. If you're someone who hasn't plotted a book before, it could be tempting to go with your first idea and rush through this so you can start drafting your story. But resist that impulse because your first ideas are not usually the best.

Remember, there are reader expectations for every genre so you can't abandon them entirely, but you can innovate—get creative. That's what writers do. That's the fun of storytelling.

For example, in our postapocalyptic trilogy, *BARREN*, the protagonist is, in fact, a "lone cowboy" which conforms to reader expectations. But instead, I introduced a "lone cowgirl." And without spoiling the story, there are several more layers to my female protagonist.

For fans of postapocalyptic science fiction, they get a lone protagonist not wanting to get involved with the world (the convention), but they get a different flavor of that character in that the protagonist is a woman (the innovation).

This is your task in creating the 12 Stages. The same but different.

What should the 12 Stages look like? The way you develop these will come down to personal taste, but I have several recommendations for the process if you're not sure where to begin.

My personal favorite (before putting them into the work-sheet)—and I'll get into more details about this in World—is to use index cards or sticky notes.

My co-writer and business partner, Zach, lives in Nashville, and I live in Cleveland. That makes Cincinnati about halfway between us. Every few months we meet there to have company and story meetings. I always pack a roll of blue painter's tape and a stack of sticky notes. We use the tape to make three columns on the wall, and then each sticky note represents one of the 12 Stages. This allows us to move them around, rearrange the ideas physically, and see them all before us. When we're finished with our meetings, we take a picture and save that file for easy reference when we're back at our respective desks weeks or months later.

Once you're satisfied with your 12 Stages, it's time to transfer them onto your Three Story Method worksheet in the "Structure" section. A story, by definition, is a sequence of events. As the author, you must decide the order of the scenes. And even if the way you're telling the story isn't perfectly chronological, such as inserting flashback scenes into the manuscript, you must still sequence the scenes for the reader.

You can create a set of 12 Stages for other characters. Genres with shared protagonists or dual-protagonists (like romance) can benefit from doing the 12 Stages exercise for each primary character. And even single-protagonist stories could be greatly improved by examining 12 Stages from the perspective of the antagonist.

However, start with the basics. No matter what the situation or the number of protagonists, as the author, you must pick one to anchor the rest, and that should be the exercise you've just completed.

Once you have the 12 Stages, you could do the same exercise for other characters. And some of those scenes might be the same for each character. Just be aware that it does complicate matters, especially when you begin work on the outline or first-drafting.

GENRE

What is genre?

In speaking of Diction in *Poetics*, Aristotle addresses the idea of genre and how you can deliver on a reader's specific expectations.

"The perfection of style is to be clear without being mean. The clearest style is that which uses only current or proper words...witness the poetry of Cleophon and of Sthenelus. That diction, on the other hand, is lofty and raised above the commonplace which employs unusual words. By unusual, I mean strange (or rare) words, metaphorical, lengthened—anything, in short, that differs from the normal idiom...So, again, if we take a strange (or rare) word, a metaphor, or any similar mode of expression, and replace it by the current or proper term, the truth of our observation will be manifest."

If you're thinking, "My story is completely unique. It's never been told before," you are wrong. There is no such thing as a unique story. Depending on what theory you entertain, there have only been 7-12 stories ever told in the history of the world.

For example, *Star Wars: A New Hope* is not a unique story. Lucas studied and even worked with Joseph Campbell to incorporate Hero's Journey archetypes that had been used since antiquity. In fact, some even claim that *Star Wars* is a Western that takes place in outer space. The story itself is not unique but how Lucas told it certainly is.

What makes your story unique is *how* you tell a familiar story. And the way you tell it, the rules you follow, that's called *genre*.

More recently in the world of independent publishing, genre has come to be defined through the commercialization of the product. In other words, what *market* should the author target? Which commercial genre?

The phrase "write to market" comes up frequently in the independent publishing community, often with a negative connotation, due to a misunderstanding of what it means. Chris Fox wrote *Write to Market*, the definitive guide on the approach that says that writing to market requires the author to (1) love the genre and (2) identify a hungry audience for the genre.

It does *not* mean cashing in by writing whatever genre happens to be hot at the moment. That's not usually possible anyway because what's hot changes so quickly. And even if it were, it is not a long-term sustainable approach to becoming a career author.

Both Zach and I began our publishing careers as horror writers. We both had a fascination and mutual respect for Stephen King as well as a fondness for the evocative storytelling in the horror genre. However, as we began to learn more about the marketplace, we'd made a few discoveries: it is difficult to sustain the antagonist threat across multiple books in a series and readers, therefore, preferred stand-alone novels.

Also, especially for independent authors, stand-alone novels are difficult to market without an existing audience and therefore, sell-through to other stand-alone novels has quite a low percentage rate. Even in the world of traditional publishing, there are hundreds, maybe thousands, of cases where an author had a breakout stand-alone novel, but interest in their next book was mediocre at best. Imagine for a moment how much money J.K. Rowling would have left on the table if Harry Potter was a single novel.

Therefore, we both evolved into postapocalyptic authors where the genre isn't that different from horror but where readers both expect and demand serialized fiction, thereby increasing the viability of the work we wanted to sell.

"Marketing" book one of a six-book series has much more of an ROI potential than the same number of dollars spent marketing a stand-alone book. What's important to recognize is that we both *love* postapocalyptic fiction, even more so than horror. Writing in a genre because it's lucrative at the time won't work if you're not a fan of that genre. Readers will sense it, and you will burn out.

Therefore, knowing fans want military science fiction stories *and* having that as your favorite type of story to read is the perfect alignment and a good example of writing to market. Hating paranormal romance but trying to write it because you think it sells well is not writing to market. It's also not smart.

In *Save the Cat!*, Snyder looks at genre from a cinematic perspective. As we discussed in the logline exercise, Snyder wants filmmakers to be able to show the potential movie-goer what the movie is about in a matter of seconds.

"If what the movie is about isn't clear from the poster and title, what are you going to say to describe it?" Snyder believes that you must show the viewer what the movie is about through genre.

A genre mash-up is a terrible idea for most authors. While you think it's clever and will stand out, it typically confuses the reader. If you try to appeal to fans of historical romance and fans of cozy mysteries, you'll alienate both. People want more of the same but different.

For an agent to sell your manuscript to a publisher, she must be able to do so according to genre, which is the entire reason it exists in the first place.

"To anticipate the anticipations of the audience you must master your genre and its conventions." – Robert McKee

You can ignore this advice and write your cozy mystery historical romance. You'll revel in your own clever self, enjoying the intellectual freedom. Or you can choose to leverage the power of genre and get your story in front of the people who are most likely to read it, or the agents who are most likely to get it sold.

Neil Gaiman's tip is to subvert expectations. He says, "... ideas should come from two things coming together...What would happen if a werewolf bit another werewolf? What would happen if a werewolf bit a goldfish? What would happen if a werewolf bit a chair? And that is just confluence, things you have seen together a thousand times. You look at them in a slightly different way and now you have beginnings of a story."

Brian McDonald eschews the idea of genre almost completely. He wrote, "This idea may be difficult for some readers to comprehend, but I have come to understand that differences in genres are superficial and have little or no bearing on a story's power or truth. And truth is all that any story worth telling is getting at. In this regard, what I think I have discovered is the one underlying truth that links all stories...I believe that our separation of story forms is artificial and that there is almost no difference between one and another. Even the idea of fiction and nonfiction is artificial in the world of storytelling."

Genre is an interesting element of storytelling and worth thinking about as you sit down to write your story.

Use the "Genre" section of the worksheet to answer key questions to help you determine the genre.

THEME

Back in Plot, you used the Pixar Pitch and the logline approach from *Save the Cat!* to come up with an interesting story idea. At a superficial level, you've started to answer one of the most important questions regarding your story: What's it about?

But there's more work to be done because not only do you have to identify what your story is about, but you have to know what it's *really* about.

Let's start with a literal answer to that first question. Is your story about a man cheating on his spouse? Is it about robots gone wild in space? Is it about a postal worker who has a secret affinity for dogs? Remember, we need an ordinary person in an extraordinary situation. Now is when we start to flesh out that situation.

Aristotle called this Thought, which I've loosely interpreted as Theme.

He wrote, "Third in order is Thought—that is, the faculty of saying what is possible and pertinent in given circumstances. In the case of oratory, this is the function of the Political art and of the art of rhetoric."

It all starts with a desire for your protagonist. She *must* need and want something. Whether those driving forces are physical, emotional, spiritual, or psychological doesn't matter. A story must have conflict and change, and a character who is perfectly content with his situation in life is not the genesis of a story.

In Neil Gaiman's MasterClass, he also stresses the importance of knowing what the story is about because his goal is to get the reader thinking, "What's next?" Gaiman's suggestion is to write conflict based on what characters want.

Brian McDonald has the most poignant and spiritual take on the subject, which he explores in his book, *The Golden Theme*. He describes theme as an "armature" which is meant to "hold up" every element in the story. He argues that there is really only one theme that we all recognize.

"Throughout history every great person, movement, or cause has evoked the Golden Theme and operates in the world with it as a guiding principle, saying, 'We are all the same' or 'We are in this together.'"

Elaborating, McDonald wrote, "Stories may have individual themes, such as, 'there is no honor among thieves' or 'slow and steady wins the race.' But underneath all stories, no matter what their intentional theme may be, lies another message—a universal message... This simple sentence, that we are all the same, is the Golden Theme that all stories express. And it is my firm belief that the closer a story comes to illuminating this truth, the more powerful and universal it becomes, and the more people are touched by it."

Regardless of how you decide to tell a story, it all comes down to the same question. What's it about? Once you know what it's about, then you can ask, what's it *really* about?

Steven Pressfield has written extensively on theme. Although it's not always possible to know your book's theme before you begin writing it, you'd better know it by the time you finish.

Star Wars is about the Empire's quest to conquer the galaxy. But *Star Wars* is really about Luke Skywalker's maturation from a boy into a young man. Without the Internal genre, *Star Wars* would still be an entertaining science fiction adventure movie, but without Luke's journey, it would have never become such an important piece of our cultural history.

McKee prefers the phrase *Controlling Idea* over *theme*. He states that the Controlling Idea must be condensed to a single sentence and "molded around one idea." McKee believes authors must express how and why life "undergoes change from one condition of existence at the beginning to another at the end."

Another angle to approach theme is through high concept. As defined by Wikipedia, "High-concept is a type of artistic work that can be easily pitched with a succinctly stated premise. It can be contrasted with low-concept, which is more concerned with character development and other subtleties that are not as easily summarized."

At the site WritersStore.com, screenwriter Steve Kaire goes into more detail by saying, "The premise or logline is the core of High Concept. My comprehensive definition of High Concept is comprised of five requirements, each of which is mandatory. The five requirements are in descending order of importance. Therefore, numbers one and two are the most important as well as the most difficult to attain. But meeting only several of the requirements is not enough. All five requirements have to be met for success in achieving the 'slam dunk' project everyone is looking for."

Kaire goes on to list the five requirements:

1. Your premise should be original and unique.
2. Your story has to have mass audience appeal.
3. Your pitch has to be story-specific.
4. The potential is obvious.
5. Your pitch should be one to three sentences long.

Building a high concept into your premise can tie into the Controlling Idea. It can be the engine running underneath your story and the element that sets it apart from all the others. And, a high concept can spark your imagination for worldbuilding which we'll discuss in an upcoming section.

Unlike some of the other aspects of Three Story Method, there isn't an easy way to chart out a theme. Many times, it'll hit you as you write. And at other times, you'll be confounded by the theme. It might even take a fellow writer or an editor to point out the theme to you. And in the best of cases, readers will come up with different themes based on their own interpretation of your story.

Keep asking yourself, "What's it *really* about?"

One technique from *Save the Cat!* can help get you thinking about this question. Snyder writes, "Somewhere in the first five minutes of a well-structured screenplay, someone (usually *not* the main character) will post a question or make a statement (usually *to* the main character) that is the theme of the movie. 'Be careful what you wish for,' this person will say or 'Pride goeth before a fall,' or 'Family is more important than money.' It won't be this obvious, it will be conversational, an offhand remark that the main character doesn't quite get at the moment—but which will have far-reaching and meaningful impact later... This statement is the movie's *thematic premise*.'"

You might struggle to find your theme, or your theme might change as you write the story. But you, as the creator, you *must* have a theme. Keep in mind that you must answer these two most critical questions, "What's it about?" and "What's it *really* about?" Fill in this section on your Three Story Method worksheet.

Read the next section to see how I deconstructed the themes of *Star Wars*.

THE THEMES OF STAR WARS

Star Wars explores multiple themes, and these can change over time and through the lens of the observer. That's what makes a theme so powerful and why we, as artists, can rarely control the impact that our work has on others because it'll be interpreted in different ways. For example, consider some of these themes:

JUST BECAUSE YOU can't see it doesn't mean it doesn't exist.

The Force shows us that there are things governing the universe that are beyond our comprehension and understanding. Like gravity, it is a central power that can't be seen, smelled, heard, or touched. With an almost religious fervor, we're shown the power of faith and why we must believe in things, even though we don't always have evidence of their existence.

WOMEN ARE AND CAN BE, as powerful as men.

The world has changed since 1977, and it's astonishing the way Lucas was ahead of his time in his portrayal of the strong, female archetype—Princess Leia. She is beautiful, smart, powerful, and strong. It is Leia who leads them out of the prison block inside the Death Star and Leia who commands the rebel resistance.

TECHNOLOGY SHOULD BE USED **with caution.**

Obi-Wan Kenobi has an ancient weapon that Han Solo makes fun of and yet, it is that weapon that Luke will come to depend on to save his life. Although not as dependable as a blaster, in the words of Solo, the "sword" doesn't jam or misfire.

LUKE'S X-WING fighter is equipped with the latest technology including R2-D2, but when it's all on the line, Luke uses the Force to hit the target and destroy the Death Star.

THE FORCE best represents the old ways, but it has had an undeniable effect on the modern world. We're shown that technology can be beneficial, but it should be used with caution.

ANCIENT HISTORY AND RITUALS MATTER.

It's clear from Luke's conversations with Obi-Wan Kenobi that Lucas built a world where the past matters. The Jedi are an ancient order, and the history and preservation of that order are paramount to the story and the key to defeating Darth Vader.

ALTHOUGH LUKE'S FATHER DIED, Kenobi takes up the responsibility of teaching Luke about the Force and how it can be used for good instead of evil, as Vader has done with the Dark Side.

IN THE "THEME" section of the worksheet, brainstorm possible answers to the question, "What's it *really* about?" Use the examples from *Star Wars* as your guide.

CHARACTER

Character is king. We've all heard it, and we know it. Readers want characters they can root for as well as characters they can hate. If you don't have a multi-dimensional protagonist and a complex force of antagonism, your story will fall flat.

Having likeable and relatable characters can endear a reader to a book, a series, or an entire world. People identify with characters, often living vicariously through them. It's important to design magnetic characters by paying attention to detail.

However, many writers succumb to Resistance, believing they need to create a detailed portfolio for each character, the author compelled to document every facet of the character's existence. Some authors feel the need to create the main character's favorite meal, recall false memories from a fictional life—like the moment of the protagonist's first kiss. All Resistance.

Patterson likes to reveal character through action. In his MasterClass, he suggests showing a character's soft side to make her more complex, in addition to humanizing the villain and making that character clever. And in his well-earned wisdom, James Patterson also suggests making pets into secondary characters.

Mr. Patterson probably picked up a tip or two on character from Mr. Aristotle.

"Character is that which reveals moral purpose, showing what kind of things a man chooses or avoids. Speeches, therefore, which do not make this manifest, or in which the speaker does not choose or avoid anything whatever, are not expressive of character. Thought, on the other hand, is found where something is proved to be, or not to be, or a general maxim is enunciated."

Aristotle believed there were four primary components to creating interesting characters. (1) Characters should be "good" or true to their nature. (2) Each character should demonstrate "propriety" relative to their defined social class, meaning their values should be consistent with a real-life person. (3) Although not clearly explaining how this would be distinct from "good" and "propriety," Aristotle suggests that a "character must be true to life." (4) Characters must act in a consistent manner relative to their own personality.

Neil Gaiman breaks character development into two basic tenets: wants and needs. He says that character wants and needs are the engine of your story.

Libbie Hawker says that characters need "a serious, big, scary, potentially life-wrecking way. When you start with a badly flawed character, the arc will be all about correcting that flaw—about your character growing into a better person, the kind of mythic hero archetype he was 'meant to be' but couldn't become until this adventure—the events of your plot—pushed him to change himself for the better."

CASTING CHARACTERS

For reasons that are grounded in science, I also believe that extensive character-building is not only a waste of time, but it can work against you, manifesting fictional people who do not act the way real ones do. It can lead to "telling" too much of your story instead of "showing" because if you spent time creating these false memories, you could be tempted to jam them into your story, even if they're not relevant, if only to justify the time you spent creating them. Avoid info dumping. Let action drive your character.

But you do need to create and prepare characters before drafting, and we will get into that process.

Hold a casting call! This exercise will start the process and provide you the foundation for building characters that work without spending needless hours on dossiers that don't serve the story.

With co-written titles, Zach usually handles the character creation. He likes to think of specific actors and "cast" them into the novel. More specifically, he casts specific actors in specific roles.

For example, casting Tom Hanks isn't going to work because Tom Hanks appeared in *Forrest Gump, Apollo 13,* and *That Thing You Do,* playing extremely different characters. Find a specific Tom Hanks role and stick with it.

With minor characters, a picture will usually suffice, as you might only want a visual reference of what the character looks like. But for the lead characters in a story, keeping in mind the specific roles of actors gives Zach more of a base from which to work.

Copy an image of your actor in that role and paste it into your worksheet. This is not a file that will ever be shared, so don't worry about trademark or copyright infringement.

The purpose of the casting call is to put an instant personality on your character, who, up until this point, was probably just a name. Underneath the image of your new cast member, jot down a few notes about that character's personality, likes and dislikes, tendencies, and history. It doesn't need to be (and shouldn't be) highly detailed. Try to stick with physical attributes and basic personality traits.

This activity shouldn't take long and will give you a place to build out the primary characters enough that you'll be able to draft, but not requiring so much energy that it pulls you away from the story. Resistance comes in many forms.

In the "Character" section of the worksheet, begin to flesh out your main characters using the following brief information:

Picture (an actor in a specific role).
Name.
Age.
Brief lists of physical traits.
Occupation.
Marital Status.
Close Family and Friends.
Enemies.
Archetype.
Special Skills.
What does your character *want?*
What does your character *need*?
What is the intention?
What is the obstacle?
What is the lie your character believes?

Again, you might not need this much information for minor characters. For instance, you might not need to worry about wants and needs of minor characters. But for your main characters, especially your protagonist, you should fill out this entire profile, but resist the temptation to go beyond the details I've suggested.

At the bottom of your character profile, leave a notes section. This is where you can add details as you're drafting, such as relevant backstory, injuries, or disabilities a character acquires throughout the story, etc.

When I need more information about the characters, I always go back to genre. I typically write the Hero's Journey archetypal story set in a postapocalyptic world. And, according to generally accepted genre conventions that I know extremely well, I understand that our protagonist should begin the story with deep flaws but then grow and change as the story progresses.

Remember: Action reveals character.

WANTS AND NEEDS

Simply identifying a specific actor in a specific role isn't enough because there's a problem—humans are not rational creatures. We're emotional and unpredictable. We like to convince ourselves that *we* make rational choices and everyone else doesn't, but that's not true. *All* humans make most of their decisions for emotional reasons rather than ones based on logic.

Therefore, you need to ask two questions about your characters: What does your protagonist *want*? What does your protagonist *need*?

K.M. Weiland suggests creating a lie the protagonist believes, "a specific belief, which you should be able to state in one short sentence." This then makes "The Thing Your Character Needs" nothing more than a realization. "In a word, the Thing Your Character Needs is the Truth. He needs the personalized antidote to his Lie."

In *The Negative Trait Thesaurus*, Angela Ackerman and Becca Puglisi say, "Wounds are often kept secret from others because embedded within them is the lie—an untruth that the character believes about himself... For example, if a man believes he is unworthy of love (the lie) because he was unable to stop his fiancée from being shot during a robbery (the wound), he may adopt attitudes, habits, and negative traits that make him undesirable to other women."

In 1949, Abe Maslow's "A Theory of Human Motivation" was published in *Psychological Review*. The paper and theory are now better known as "Maslow's Hierarchy of Needs." His theory was that human wants and needs are driven by biology, the survival mechanisms served before the more intellectual or aspirational goals.

For example, a man who is starving to death is not actively working toward his own self-actualization—he's trying to stay alive. Although the theory has some holes and Maslow himself did not come up with the pyramid, it's still a useful tool in the author's toolkit.

But identifying a character's wants and needs isn't enough because there's a problem—humans are not rational creatures. We're emotional and unpredictable.

As a professor of history, I witnessed this firsthand with my students in a course titled, "The Salem Witch Hysteria of 1692." We studied the underlying causes of this American colonial tragedy and discovered that the fear of the unknown was a root cause of the hysteria that ended up with dozens hanged or imprisoned on charges of witchcraft. No scientific evidence had ever been presented and several of the judges later acknowledged their role in the event or apologized for feeding into that fear.

Those colonists in Salem, Massachusetts, weren't stupid or

foolish—but they weren't rational. And throughout history, we've seen groups of people act in ways that are not logical.

That's why, to write convincing characters, it helps to understand how we act as humans. In fiction, we show character through action, and action is equivalent to a decision. Which may lead you to ask...

HOW WE MAKE DECISIONS

How do we make decisions?

ANALYSIS BY CHRISTINE DAIGLE, *Ph.D., C.Psych.*

Practice in Child and Adolescent Clinical Psychology and Clinical Neuropsychology

TO ANSWER THIS QUESTION, let's consider a few basic scientific concepts about how our nervous system functions. Our brain's reward and punishment system drives everything we do. Keep in mind that what's rewarding or punishing is different for each person, depending on their genetics and experiences. The following is a simple way to think about a behavior sequence, from initiation to completion.

CUE/STIMULUS	CRAVING/THREAT	RESPONSE/REACTION	REWARD/PUNISHMENT/NEUTRAL
1	2	3	4

First, we encounter a cue or stimulus. Second, our brain interprets this cue or stimulus as a threat or a craving. Third, the threat or craving gives us motivation/drive to act, and this action can be an automatic reaction or a thoughtful response. Finally, there is a result or consequence that is a reward, a punishment, or neutral feedback.

For example,

1) stimulus - we see an attractive person,

2) craving - we desire to be with that person,

3) thoughtful response - we speak to that person,

4) reward - we connect.

This same scenario could go down the punishment and neutral feedback routes. We could choose not to speak to that person. Or the outcome could be rejection.

While responding to a craving is useful, it is usually threat-related behavior that makes our characters riveting. For example,

1) stimulus – the protagonist sees the antagonist,

2) threat – the antagonist pulls a gun,

3) reaction – the protagonist takes *flight* and hides behind a brick wall,

4) reward – the protagonist avoids getting shot.

How Do We Choose an Action?

When we encounter a cue or stimulus, it evokes a response in the emotional regulatory system of the brain (limbic and paralimbic system) that generates an emotional reaction while signaling the decision-making part of the brain (prefrontal cortex). This signal says something like, "Please select strategies to either increase or decrease my current emotional state." Based on what the decision-making part of our brain tells us, we either calm down or escalate to eliminate the threat.

This process is not as well-developed in children and adolescents. Children really can't self-regulate the way adults do as these brain systems are still maturing into our twenties. These systems are incomplete by design.

How Do We Respond to a Threat?

The anatomical connection between our emotional regulation area and decision-making areas developed recently in terms of our evolution. It's like a highway of information that is easily shut down when there's an accident. When a threat produces a significant-enough reaction, our emotional reptile brain disconnects from our primate decision-making brain, and we enter fight, flight, or freeze.

As a result, we don't make rational decisions when the threat is significant. We act based on a quick evaluation combined with our default reaction of fight/flight/freeze. It is useful to think about this when determining your character's actions both in general and at specific times. Is he a person who will most often fight, take flight, or freeze? In the particular scene you're writing, will the character choose his default reaction, or will the nature of the threat make him choose differently?

Why Do We Respond to Threats This Way?

It comes out of a desire to avoid pain. Through our evolution, our brains were designed to help us survive and pass on our genes. This means that a long time ago, the people who survived were the ones who were always scanning their environment for threats. We have developed an automatic bias to look for danger. Even though no tiger is likely to jump out of the shadows, we scan our world for past mistakes we can't afford to repeat and future threats we want to avoid and be prepared to deal with, which is explored more deeply in "Learning to Be Present With Yourself," an article in *Psychology Today*.

Wants and Needs

The reactive or rational basis for our actions is related to, but not exactly the same as, assessing our wants and needs. Our circumstances in life can be transitory, and with life changes come changes in wants and needs. What we want and what we need may be the same thing (food), or they may be different things (e.g., we want a new car, but we need love and belonging). Therefore, you need to ask two questions of your characters: What does your protagonist want? What does your protagonist need? While what your character needs may change from scene to scene, your character should also have a main, overarching need.

Human Needs Are Driven by Biology

In his 1943 paper, *A Theory of Human Motivation*, psychologist Abraham Maslow posited that human beings have an inborn step-by-step "hierarchy of needs." For storytelling, this is a useful categorization of needs. Once you satisfy a low-level need, you move to the next level. Once you have that satisfied, you go up to another level and then another until you reach the top. The hierarchy begins at a strictly physical level and progresses to a metaphysical (internal) level.

Physiological Needs

These are biological requirements necessary for survival: For example, air, food, water, sleep, sex, clothing, warmth, shelter. If we do not meet these needs, the human body can't function properly.

Safety Needs

Safety is the next level of need. This includes protection from elements, defending the shelter, security, order, law, stability, easing hostilities with other human beings, and freedom from fear.

Love (Affiliation and Belongingness)

This is the need for interpersonal relationships. It includes intimacy, communication, sharing experiences, finding a mate, family communion, friendship, trust, acceptance, receiving and giving love and affection, affiliating, and being part of a group (family, friends, work). Types of love include a mother's love, a father's love, sibling love, the larger sphere of family love, romantic love, and being loved by society.

Esteem

There are two types of esteem:

1) Self-esteem is represented by confidence, coming to an

understanding of one's place in society and finding contentment, self-satisfaction, dignity, achievement, mastery, and independence.

2) Desire for reputation or respect from others (e.g., status, prestige) such as your partner, family, and society at large. Reputation is often a primary need for adolescents.

Cognitive Needs

Presented as knowledge and understanding, curiosity, exploration, and need for meaning and predictability.

Aesthetic Needs

Put forward as appreciation and search for beauty, balance, and form.

Self-Actualization

This is a desire to become everything one is capable of being or expressing an inner gift.

It includes realizing personal potential, self-fulfillment, and seeking personal growth and peak experiences.

Transcendence

A category added at the end of Maslow's life, transcendence occurs when a person is motivated by values that transcend beyond the personal self (e.g., mystical experiences and certain experiences with nature, aesthetic experiences, sexual experiences, service to others, the pursuit of science, religious faith, etc.) This occurs when people stop thinking about themselves and share themselves with the greater world. They derive satisfaction from doing things for other people instead of obtaining satisfaction from their own creative efforts. It is using a gift for the pleasure of other people with no ulterior motive.

Updated Hierarchy of Needs

In 2010, Kenrick et al. published a paper in *Perspectives on Psychological Sciences* updating Maslow's Hierarchy of Needs. While the changes in categories are more important from a scientific perspective, a useful change for storytellers is Kenrick et al.'s hypothesis that higher-level needs overlap with, rather than completely replace, lower-level needs. Once a level is achieved, it can be triggered whenever that need becomes important.

As stated above, action defines character (and action is decision). Defining wants and needs will help clarify which action your character will choose.

USING THE CHARACTER SHEET

So, when you're working on the worksheet in the "Character" section, it's best to pay close attention to *Wants* and *Needs*.

These can appear to be the same thing, but differentiating between the two will make your characters deeper and richer.

For example, Luke Skywalker *wants* the waiting to end, to get off of Tatooine and go somewhere more exciting than where he grew up (typical teenager). But what he needs is a challenge, to grow beyond the yeoman farmer lot he's been cast and share his gift with the greater world (transcendence).

At the beginning of the movie, we can see how Luke's wants and needs are related but different. And it's clear that on Luke's journey to satisfy his overarching need, he masters each of Maslow's tiered goals along the way.

In *The Writer's Journey*, Vogler writes, "Through the triggering device of wishes, stories seem to like arranging events so that the hero is forced to evolve to a higher level of awareness. Often the hero wishes for something that she or he desperately *wants* at that moment, but the story teaches the hero to look beyond, to what he or she really *needs*."

VOGLER HAS COME up with a simple device to help authors teach the hero the needed lesson—NOBA, which stands for, "Not Only... But Also." This device is common in fortune-telling systems such as tarot. Vogler says it means (speaking to the hero), "Here is a truth that you know perfectly well, but there is another dimension to this truth of which you may not be aware."

MASLOW'S HIERARCHY and the Hero's Journey archetypes help us drill down to character motivation, which is the Holy Grail of characterization because if we know what is driving the main character's behavior, the choices she makes will reveal her character.

IT INCORPORATES NOT ONLY her past experiences but her personality traits and present values. And all of this is without needing to know her favorite color or the name of her third-grade teacher, which you might be tempted to spend time developing in an extensive character dossier.

IN *THE ART of War for Writers*, James Scott Bell wrote a chapter titled, "The key to reader bonding is falling in love with the Lead." In it, Bell believes that there are only a few things you need to know to get readers loving your characters.

1. Great characters have grit, wit, and it.
2. Character is revealed in crisis.
3. You should know the character's deepest thoughts, yearnings, secrets, and fears.
4. Emotionally bond the reader to the character.

AND IN THE SUBSEQUENT CHAPTER, Bell stresses the need to "deploy a character who reveals both inner struggle and inner conflict." Bell writes, "An *inner struggle* is something the Lead brings with her into the story... The *inner conflict* is a product of the plot. It is the 'argument' the character is having inside over the pursuit of the objective."

OTHER THAN THE simple photograph and physical description for your characters, what else do you need?

JOSEPH CAMPBELL IDENTIFIED character archetypes into the Hero's Journey framework that not only serve the global story but provide the author with a canvas on which to paint these fictional folks.

VOGLER TOOK IT A STEP FURTHER, dedicating his entire Book

1 of *The Writer's Journey* to detail these roles that must be fulfilled. Vogler believes writers should keep in mind these two critical questions when trying to identify the nature of an archetype: What psychological function or part of the personality does it represent and what is its dramatic function in the story?

VOGLER'S ARCHETYPES

Here's a summary of Vogler's archetypes for *Star Wars: A New Hope*:

Hero (Luke Skywalker)

In Greek, the word hero means, "to protect and to serve." The protagonist of your story should be the hero if your story is an Internal Genre as defined by Coyne in *Story Grid*. The hero is someone—male or female—who will make some sacrifice on behalf of the greater good. And during the process, the hero will learn something about self or the world at large. This is the main character, the protagonist, the character with whom you want your reader to bond.

Mentor (Obi-Wan Kenobi)

Often the Wise Old Man or Wise Old Woman, this arche-type's job is to protect and teach the hero. Mentor helped

Telemachus in Homer's *The Odyssey,* and since then, the word has come to mean "helper," or "guide."

THRESHOLD GUARDIAN (The Death Star)

Although sometimes a force of antagonism, the Threshold Guardian exists to challenge those who are not worthy, warning them away from crossing a *threshold* into another time or space. The Threshold Guardian may challenge the Hero and even be a minor lieutenant of the villain. And in some cases, the Hero can turn the Threshold Guardian into an Ally.

HERALD (R2-D2's MESSAGE, the general briefing when the pilots are about to attack the Death Star)

The Herald issues challenges to the Hero and marks the coming of significant change in the story. The all-important "Call to Adventure" in Campbell's theory is usually delivered by the Herald who can explain the challenge to the Hero—and the reader.

SHAPESHIFTER (HAN SOLO)

From the Hero's perspective, the Shapeshifter is difficult to pin down. As the name implies, this character archetype has a shifting and unstable nature. Vogler believes that the Shapeshifter is often a member of the opposite sex "whose primary characteristic is that they appear to change constantly from the hero's point of view." A Shapeshifter can be an Ally or a Shadow, and often will change roles throughout the story.

SHADOW (DARTH VADER)

The Shadow represents the force of darkness, "the unexpressed, unrealized, or rejected aspects of something." Villains, enemies, and antagonists are imbued with the spirit of the Shadow. In some cases, the Shadow wants death and destruction, an urge to destroy rather than create. However, the Shadow can appear as a struggle within the Hero or as an Ally who fundamentally disagrees with what the Hero believes.

ALLY (HAN SOLO, Princess Leia, R2-D2, C-3PO)

Every Hero needs an Ally. This archetype "can serve a variety of necessary functions, such as companion, sparring partner, conscience, or comic relief." An Ally can be a friend or sidekick of the Hero, becoming a sounding board for the Hero while also running errands or handling other mundane tasks.

TRICKSTER (HAN SOLO, C-3PO, R2-D2)

The Trickster usually shows up as a clown, comedic sidekick, or practical jokester. The archetype "embodies the energies of mischief and desire for change." The Trickster also helps to humanize the Hero, often poking fun at the Hero to humanize her and signal to the audience that the

Hero has flaws. The Trickster reminds the reader, and the Hero, not to take ourselves so seriously.

A NOTE on archetypes from Vogler. He writes, "There are, of course, many more archetypes; as many as there are human qualities to dramatize in stories... Particular genres of modern stories have their specialized character types... However, these are only variants and refinements of the archetypes..."

IT IS important to note that the archetypes are most useful when interpreted as *roles* versus *characters*. The roles of characters can change throughout a story, and the source of antagonism can shift as well. A character can start as a Mentor, become a Shapeshifter, and then end the story as a Shadow.

USING *STAR WARS* AS AN EXAMPLE, Darth Vader begins as a Shadow and eventually (spoiler alert) turns into Luke's Mentor. In another example from Lucas' masterpiece, the Force is literally a force, and when wielded by Darth Vader, it, too, can become a Shadow.

NOW IT'S time to go back to your Three Story Method worksheet. Begin to cast other characters and do your best to mold them from one of the eight archetypes. This worksheet should be kept close at hand, allowing you to add to it easily.

. . .

IF YOU GET STUCK DETERMINING a character's role or their arc, reference the archetypes. Also, go back to genre, as your answer could be found there. With the help of the book, *Story Arcana* by Caroline Donahue, Zach has used tarot to develop characters, whether it's studying the artwork to help him visualize how a character should look, or by digging deeper into the card's meaning to discover a character's wants and needs. You can find out more about using tarot in storytelling by checking the Appendix.

WORLD

"The poet being an imitator, like a painter or any other artist, must of necessity imitate one of three objects—things as they were or are, things as they are said or thought to be, or things as they ought to be." Aristotle, *Poetics*

The world of the story, especially for fiction writers, can be an enticing siren. It's easy to be consumed by the magical and exciting prospect of playing God—of creating a universe from your own imagination.

However, too much time spent here can be harmful. World-building can be a form of Resistance in disguise.

In her book, *Storyworld First*, Jill Williamson stresses, "Your first goal is to entertain your reader. You may have created the coolest storyworld ever, but if you don't have amazing characters and a gripping plot, no one will likely care."

Whether you're writing fiction or nonfiction, you must begin the process with this simple statement:

Something is wrong with the world.

It could be that it's impossible to lose weight while eating only chocolate-covered kale, or that dragons are overrunning Lord Hiforth's castle. In whatever form your story takes, you must have conflict. And one way to help create conflict is to design a flawed universe.

Without a force of antagonism, the protagonist has no mission, and therefore, there is no story. Whatever is wrong in the world should directly threaten the main character's safety or well-being. But to have a truly engaging story, that threat should extend to a group within society or an entire civilization.

When Zach and I decided to form Molten Universe Media, we knew we would need something wrong with the world we'd created for our first series. Both of us had spent time in New Orleans, and we love the city. In August of 2005, Zach was living only a couple of hours away from New Orleans when Hurricane Katrina hit, and had long wanted to reflect on some of his personal experiences with the storm through his fiction. Hurricane Katrina had changed much in that region of the country, and we thought, what if there wasn't any coming back from that? And, what if a supernatural force had been hiding in the French Quarter, waiting to take advantage of the natural disaster?

Hence, the world of our *Final Awakening* series was born.

Superhero stories are based on a world in peril, usually at the hands of an evil villain. Self-help books are based on a world that appears too fast and complicated to manage on one's own. Children's books are based on threats to innocence, happiness, and contentment.

In *Star Wars*, we have the Imperial Empire trying to crush

the rebellion in a world torn between the powers of light and dark as symbolized through the Force.

The protagonist should face a major Choice that has consequences for more than his own life. Although not every project will require a life-and-death situation, any time you can raise the stakes on the problem in your universe, the reader will be inextricably drawn in. The entire planet does not need to hang in the balance, but a force in the world should pose a dire and immediate threat to the protagonist.

Genre plays a critical role in determining how much worldbuilding you should do. If you're writing contemporary romance, your worldbuilding document will probably be short, even if it involves creating a fictional town. But if you're writing an epic space adventure, such as *Star Wars*, then there are more elements to create to make the world immersive.

But beware of Resistance. Too many times I've seen authors spend weeks or months on a worldbuilding document—crafting a society, social classes, history, language, races, and more. In certain genre fiction, such as epic fantasy, this is not only required but will be demanded by the readers of the genre.

The extent and level of detail involved should be balanced with the amount of time spent *not* writing. Only writing is writing, and it's easy to rationalize the time spent on worldbuilding as making progress on the project.

This is also why worldbuilding happens this late in the Three Story Method process. By the time you're ready to build your world, you should know the kind of story you're going to tell. This will allow you to focus on the worldbuilding elements that matter most, as opposed to building out a fictional world without first knowing how you're going to use it.

You could be tempted to skip the previous levels and build your story world first. And as we discussed with characters, that could lead to you forcing things into your story, if only because you took the time to create them. It's important to remember that lightsabers, the Force, and the reason for Tatooine's two suns, mean nothing without Luke's already established arc.

BUILDING THE WORLD

To prevent that delightful slide into your fictional universe, focus on the four primary elements of worldbuilding:

1. Characters.

2. Setting.

3. Timeline.

4. Rules.

CHARACTERS

WE'VE ALREADY COVERED characters and characterization extensively, so let's move into setting.

. . .

Setting

GENRE WILL BE the most important determining factor when it comes to setting. Create the setting early in the story creation process, about the same time as the 12 Stages, because the location of the story should impact the types of obstacles the protagonist will face.

REMEMBER, something must be wrong in this universe because that will be the underlying motivation for the characters. Factors such as terrain, weather, and population can have important ramifications when it comes to your plot.

IT CAN BE easy to develop familiar surroundings without ever having been to the location through the use of the Internet, online maps, and photographs. An even better approach would be to visit the physical location where the story takes place to familiarize yourself with local customs and idiosyncrasies.

YOU CAN ALSO CREATE a fictional town, modeling it after a real location but allowing yourself to be creative with the details. Stephen King famously did this with his fictional American town of Derry, Maine, which he has used as a setting in several of his stories.

ROBERT MCKEE DEFINES setting in terms of being four-dimensional. *Period* is a story's place in time. *Duration* is a story's length through time. *Location* is a story's place in space. *Level of conflict* is the story's position on the hierarchy of human struggles.

USING THESE DEFINITIONS, creating a single-page quadrant and describing the terms can help organize the world you've created.

Period	Location
Duration	Level of Conflict

Timeline

KEEPING track of the story's timeline is critical when it comes to creating an authentic reader experience.

FOR EXAMPLE, if your character has a meal in a specific restaurant in your universe, make sure that restaurant is operating in the real world, in the timeline you've established, or readers will cry foul. However, minute-by-minute timelines are not necessary.

AGAIN, writing in a genre such as epic fantasy can require a more detailed timeline. However, events that don't impact the protagonist or are not relevant to the plot do not need to be created and chronicled. The simple version of the timeline should include the beginning and end point for the main character as well as significant events you've plotted in between.

Events or situations that have occurred off-screen can be included on the timeline and make a good reference for you as the author, but trying to shoehorn those into your story to justify the time you spent creating them will slow the pace and ultimately leave readers bored.

Rules

Universe rules vary by genre. Speculative fiction, memoir, and literary fiction create a different reading experience. Stories set in a contemporary world don't need rules at all, provided the reader understands what's wrong inside of it. These problems could (and often do) mirror issues or concerns in the present.

But the commercial genre of urban fantasy, for example, requires a specific set of rules as they apply to magic. The reader will suspend disbelief as part of the contract between the author and fantasy reader, but those rules need to be clear. In a fictional universe, as well as in our universe, physics must adhere to whatever laws the author has created. If the fire burns blue in a fantastic world, then it should always burn blue in that world.

Although books and movies are different mediums with

different expectations and experiences, analysis of movies can often be enlightening for authors. To illustrate the appropriate level of worldbuilding authors should consider, let's take another look at *Star Wars: A New Hope,* released in 1977.

THE WORLD OF STAR WARS

As stated on IMDB.com, "Luke Skywalker joins forces with a Jedi Knight, a cocky pilot, a Wookiee and two droids to save the galaxy from the Empire's world-destroying battle station, while also attempting to rescue Princess Leia from the mysterious Darth Vader."

CHARACTERS

THE WORLD IS LARGE, but the cast is relatively small, the focus on a core group of characters with Luke Skywalker as the protagonist. Obi-Wan, Han Solo, Chewbacca, C-3PO, R2-D2, and Princess Leia all help the young Jedi on his hero's journey.

LUCAS TAKES great care to introduce us to these characters without unnecessary exposition. In dialogue—especially between Obi-Wan and Luke—we discover the long and ancient history of this world. Over several films, the histories of each character are slowly revealed.

Setting

"A LONG TIME ago in a galaxy far, far away...."

PROBABLY THE MOST succinct and recognized setting in all of cinematic history. We know immediately that this is a space-traveling futurist world, but it doesn't exist in our time. Humans have mastered intergalactic travel, have worked with and fought against alien civilizations, and it's a world in which an all-powerful spirit controls everything—the Force.

Period - A long time ago.	Location - A galaxy far, far away.
Duration - A few months?	Level of Conflict - The battle between good and evil.

Timeline

THE STORY TAKES place over a few weeks. Events come fast and furious as Luke is propelled through his Hero's Journey. We don't know much about when the rebellion began or why, although that is explored further in the prequel movies, Episodes 1, 2, and 3. For this movie, that history isn't necessary and doesn't show up on the screen.

Rules

.   .   .

IN THIS SCIENCE fiction world of the past, the rules are somewhat conventional with one exception. Humans have mastered spaceflight and advanced weaponry, the technology so advanced that the Imperial Death Star rivals a planetary satellite.

AN INNOVATION of the genre is the use of the Force, giving the world a real sense of mysticism and supernatural elements.

LUCAS TIES the world to the plot in the way the characters use the weapons. Luke destroys the Death Star not with the advanced weaponry of the rebellion but by tuning into his Zen-like connection with the Force.

THE COMBINATION of fantastical and real-world elements of the world help to make *Star Wars: A New Hope* both unique and engaging.

GETTING STARTED IN YOUR WORLD

In his MasterClass, Gaiman believes in specificity. He says, "Smuggle the real world into your fictional one."

WEILAND SUGGESTS a character motivation that should underlie the rules of the world. "The Normal World is a place the protagonist either doesn't want to leave or can't leave. It's the staging ground for his grand adventure."

IN SUMMARY, enjoy creating a universe to house your story but create only enough to tell the protagonists' tale. While we enjoy worldbuilding and extensive character bios, histories, and settings, readers do not unless it's a genre with those expectations, such as epic fantasy.

CREATE ONLY what you need and let the readers' imagination do the rest.

. . .

IN THE "WORLD" section of your worksheet, fill out Robert McKee's Setting Dimensions and list any rules unique to your world.

PART III

WHAT'S NEXT

PANTS OR OUTLINE

"When forced to work within a strict framework the imagination is taxed to its utmost—and will produce its richest ideas. Given total freedom the work is likely to sprawl." – T.S. Eliot

How do you proceed? Now that you've looked at all of the components of Three Story Method, what do you do next?

I believe you should make a plan before anything else.

Only writing is writing, which means your inclination to jump into the first draft and get going is perfectly natural. The words in that draft will eventually create the story while the other words in the project probably won't.

In Plot and Structure, you've taken a raw idea and created a pitch, logline, and created the most basic of your story elements. Then, you developed the three-act structure and 12 Stages. Next, you determined who wants to read your story and what it's really about in Genre and Theme. Finally, you developed your cast in Character and set the rules for your imaginary universe in World.

Now it's time to pull out your completed worksheet, which will guide you through the drafting process and beyond. Without it, you're like a contractor without architectural drawings, throwing up walls and framing doors haphazardly and without intention. The structure might be a house, or it might be a pile of construction material.

If you don't have a plan, it's more likely to turn into a pile of construction material.

This belief has been the spark of many debates among writers, for years, maybe decades. In the introduction, we discussed the plotter vs. pantser debate and now, it's time to revisit it to take a closer look at why career authors plot or outline before sitting down to draft.

Pantsing means you're sitting at the keyboard, staring at a blank screen and hoping for the Muse to anoint you with magical storytelling dust. You have no plan because you want to be surprised or excited. Pure pantsers concealing a hint of shame call it "discovery writing," but it doesn't change what it is—risky. You could end up with a fabulous draft, but you're more likely to end up throwing out 30% to 40% of your words because the scenes or chapters don't work.

Plotters utilize Three Story Method and head into a project with a refined outline, much like a general heading into battle with a plan. Whether it's a story beat document, story spine, or outline, plotters know where they're going. The mere act of sitting in the chair and writing a scene from the outline commands the Muse.

But both of these approaches sit at the opposite ends of a

spectrum. Most writers, myself included, tend to fall somewhere in the middle.

However, I would argue that the closer you are to the plotter end, the fewer words (and time) you're going to waste. You can plot the major events of your book or story and still leave room for discovery. But if you pants a 90,000-word draft, there's no doubt you'll be spending time revising and cutting words that don't serve the story.

As I mentioned in the introduction, I'm not saying you *can't* write a good story by pantsing. But why would you gamble with precious minutes and hours you'll never get back?

If you are an experienced writer and you've successfully *finished* books, then an outline is not as critical. Once Story structure is incorporated into your creative mindset, you could use the 12 Stages as mile markers along the way without the need to map out the rest of the scenes. However, this takes time and should only be considered if you're *finishing* books.

You've made it this far in Three Story Method, which means you already understand the importance of planning before writing. It just makes sense as an author, an architect, a general, a wedding *planner*, and so on.

What the heck should be in the outline? Luckily, the Three Story Method system is fluid and flexible—easily adapted to fit your needs. Let's begin by examining some other methodologies that have influenced my work on Three Story Method.

WHAT THE PROS DO

Overall, James Patterson presents an interesting challenge to the author. He suggests building in plot twists that take your story to the unexpected.

In chapter 5 of *Save the Cat!*, Blake Snyder introduces us to The Board. He writes, "I use a big corkboard that I can hang on the wall and stare at. I like to get a pack of index cards and a box of pushpins and stick up my beats on The Board, and move 'em around at will... The Board is a way for you to 'see' your movie before you start writing... And though it is not really writing, and though your perfect plan may be totally abandoned in the white heat of actually executing your screenplay, it is on The Board where you can work out the kinks of the story before you start."

Although *Save the Cat!* was written for screenwriters, novelists can learn how to become better storytellers with Snyder's book. His description of The Board reminds us that movies aren't "pantsed."

The Board is one way to outline the story before writing the words. Also, The Board (and the outline) are not written in stone. The outline is meant to give you direction in the drafting, not restrict your innate creativity.

In *Story*, McKee calls it a "Step-Outline." He suggests using one- or two-sentence statements simply explaining what happens in the scene and how it turns. He even suggests putting the Step-Outline on cards.

The Three Story Method outline is a fusion and adaptation of techniques from other methodologies.

McKee writes, "STORY VALUES are the universal qualities of human experience that may shift from positive to negative, or negative to positive, from one moment to the next." McKee believes that conflict and change are at the heart of Story and polarity shift is how that change is measured.

Christopher Vogler believes polarity is critical in any story. He writes, "Polarity is an essential principle of storytelling, governed by a few simple rules but capable of generating infinite conflict, complexity, and audience involvement... Polarities in stories form a conceptual framework with which to organize ideas and energy, building up positive and negative charges around selected characters, words, and concepts."

While the Hero's Journey provides the higher order intellectual reasoning for the need for polarity in a story, Coyne brings it down to the practical level in *Story Grid*. He believes that each and every scene must turn on a life value and that the life value needs to be polarizing.

When conflict arises and the energy changes from positive to negative, or negative to positive, or negative to double negative, the scene turns and therefore works—keeping readers turning pages.

"The effect of a beautifully turned moment is that filmgoers experience a rush of knowledge *as if they did it for themselves.*" – Robert McKee

Coyne writes, "A scene must move from one value state to another. From a positive expression of a value like 'love' to a negative expression of that value 'hate.'

"The most dangerous mistake a writer can make is to write a scene where 'nothing happens.' We think something is happening in every scene we draft, but if you can't find a polarity shift, you can rest assured nothing has happened.

"The most important thing to remember about writing a scene is that it has to TURN. It has to move from one state of being to another. It can be a subtle turn, but it must turn in a meaningful way."

As you can see, both Vogler and Coyne see the importance of shifting polarity and turning a scene.

STARTING THE OUTLINE

I use a simple format to create the outline. It should consist of several key elements that address who, what, when, where, why, and how.

Who

In a multiple POV story, this is absolutely critical, but it helps in single POV stories as well. On your outline, indicate from which POV the scene is being told *and* who is in the scene. You might think you're giving your primary protagonist the lion's share of the scenes, but if you color code the "POV" on your outline, you'll easily be able to tally the number of scenes and adjust accordingly.

What

During your story, especially if your protagonist is on a journey, she will likely obtain and lose items along the way.

Shuffling through your notes can slow your momentum and therefore, it's worth keeping a list of items possessed by each character in the scene.

WHEN

Nothing will frustrate you more in revisions than having to go back and fix timing issues. If the sun rises in a scene that lasts an hour, it can't be dark in the next. The story becomes so ingrained in your head that it's easy to lose track of time.

THEREFORE, don't. Always put a time stamp on every scene of the outline. Even if you're never going to reveal the month, the days of the week, or the elapsed time to the reader, include it for your own sake. I like to pick calendar dates to make sure the timing doesn't drift on me.

WHERE

Simply stated, where does the scene take place? Be as specific as possible. Include the setting (like "in a house" or "at the river") while also including the location (like "London" or "the South Side of Chicago"). If your story never leaves a particular town or city, you probably don't need to include the city-level location for each scene. In that case, drilling down to neighborhood locations might be more useful.

As SHAWN COYNE SAYS OFTEN, "universality through specificity" meaning, the more specific your details, the more others can relate to and internalize your story. Don't be afraid to get as specific as possible, even if you never plan on revealing the exact names of those locations to readers.

WHY

Why is this scene in your manuscript? If it is not advancing the plot or revealing character, it should be cut.

HOW

How does the character get out of the situation you've put her in? If you can't identify how a scene begins and ends in 2-3 sentences, you will probably struggle to do so in 1,500-2,000 words.

IF YOU PUT it all together, you'll end up with an outline populated by scene descriptions that look like this:

SCENE 12 // day 78 // Luke POV // the Death Star // night // space

Conflict: On his way to the Millennium Falcon to escape the Death Star, Luke hears lightsabers.

Choice: Should he intervene in the fight and save Ben but give up Leia, or does he leave Ben to a certain death to escape the Death Star with Leia to save the Rebellion?

Consequence: Ben is killed by Darth Vader. Luke leaves with Han Solo, Princess Leia, and crew.

. . .

THAT BEAT IS 70 WORDS. If you have about 70 scenes in your novel, the word count of the beats will total about 4,900 words. If you plan on writing an 80,000-word book, you're still "pantsing" 84% of the novel—enough to make most pantsers happy.

IF YOU DON'T WANT to be that specific, or if you want to leave space for the Muse, consider using *scene seeds* which are a few simple beats to get you into the scene. You need a scene starter, a decision, and an outcome.

USING the example above from *Star Wars*:

Conflict = trapped on the Death Star

Choice = save Ben or get Leia to safety

Consequence = Ben dies but they escape

KEEP it simple and to the point, and allow room to explore and surprise yourself within the scene. I will agree with pantsers on one point—a comprehensive outline is incredibly exhausting, and will bore you and the reader.

CHALLENGE yourself to write a scene summary of a few sentences that you'll then turn into 1,500-2,000 words that will make even the Muse weep tears of joy. And remember, the outline is a *plan*, not the final draft. You likely will, and at times *should*, deviate from it as you write the story. In the drafting phase, if you think one of those scenes on the outline is boring or doesn't work, get rid of it.

LOOK AT THE "PLANNING" section of the worksheet and begin writing scene summaries, one at a time.

BEFORE DRAFTING

"The first draft of anything is shit." – Ernest Hemingway

You've taken your best idea and leveled up, put a plan in place, and you're ready to go. Congratulations! And now, the real work begins...

The first draft can be daunting, and many novels have died on the vine of those early, blank pages. But you've given yourself the best shot at success because you've done all the preparations. Like a general ready to head into battle, your troops are trained and disciplined.

There isn't a magic pill or secret method of writing a first draft. It comes down to butt in the chair. Whether you write by hand, type, or dictate your words, the most difficult part of the journey awaits—but it's also the most exciting.

In the first draft, you'll write with confidence based on what you've developed in Three Story Method, but you'll also discover hidden gems of your subconscious that find their way into the story. People, experiences, and emotions will rise to the surface and fill your mind in unique and exciting ways.

Make sure to enjoy the process, but get those words out as fast as possible. I believe that the faster you write, the easier the drafting becomes. Don't try to make every page perfect before moving to the next. Remember, that's what you'll do in revisions. Get the story out of your head. Try to write every day until the draft is finished. It doesn't matter if that takes you 6 weeks, 6 months, or 6 years, as long as you're writing every single day. Once you step away from a draft, you begin to lose the magic gossamer and Resistance becomes stronger. And in those writing sessions, write to a time limit or word count but don't stop until you've hit it.

You'll feel alone, frustrated, and want to give up. You'll become excited, ecstatic, and think you've written the best scene in the history of modern literature. And then you'll have those exact same thoughts tomorrow.

Just. Don't. Stop.

The same holds true if you're writing nonfiction because a story is a story. Writing nonfiction can tend to take longer because there's often research involved. Try to keep as much of that out of the drafting phase as possible, or if you must research, do it in a different designated time block.

Remember, you want to draft hard and fast. If Hemingway thought his first drafts were shit, you can rest easily knowing yours will be, too.

After you're done drafting

Story Grid is the single-most powerful and comprehensive revision tool available today. Shawn Coyne spent decades developing his methodology as an acquisitions editor for New York City publishers. I owe a great debt to Shawn for becoming my teacher and mentor. To this day, I run every manuscript I finish through Story Grid to make sure the story works, even after doing pre-production with Three Story Method.

Just because you use Three Story Method to draft and Story Grid to revise doesn't mean you'll crank out a *New York Times* bestseller or earn thousands in royalties from your book, but you will create a story that works—you'll have readers wanting more.

Finally, it's important to remember that there is no one way to write. Three Story Method is one methodology among many that can help you to achieve your goal of writing that first draft.

Frazzled over your draft? **Can't figure out what to do next?**

We're considering a weekend workshop called, "From Over-whelmed to Outline in 48 Hours." Imagine showing up with nothing on Friday afternoon and having a plan in place for drafting on Monday morning.

THREE**STORY**
METHOD

https://thecareerauthor.com/3smworkshoprequest/

If that is something you'd be interested in attending, please click on the link and let us know. You're not obligated by doing so and expressing your interest will help us determine if we'll host the event.

ACKNOWLEDGMENTS

I'd like to show my sincere appreciation to the contributors and experts who helped define *Three Story Method* including but not limited to James R. Essien, Christine Daigle, Christopher Wills, Kim Hudson, Marc Graham, K.M. Weiland, and Caroline Donahue.

SPECIAL SHOUT out to Seth Godin for taking time out of his busy day to answer my question.

THANKS to all of the early readers who gave me crucial feedback, including the wickedly smart Crys Cain who has an eye for detail.

AS ALWAYS, I couldn't do this without our amazingly talented and thorough editor, Eve Paludan. She always takes my writing to the next level.

. . .

AND OF COURSE, my partner in crime and cowriter, fellow metal head and brother from another mother, Zach Bohannon. I love you, man!

I HATE acknowledgements because I always forget people. Apologies for those I may have inadvertently left out.

PART IV

APPENDIX

ABOUT THE APPENDIX

In this appendix, you'll find more resources to help you make the most out of Three Story Method, including a works cited page listing all of the books, classes, and methodologies I've researched. Also included is a printable version of the Three Story Method worksheet referenced throughout the book.

TABLE OF CONTENTS

LINKS & Resources - https://
thecareerauthor.com/3smlinksandresources/

- Three Story Method worksheet
- "Temple of the Dogs" Three Story Method
  worksheet

AN INTERVIEW WITH KIM HUDSON

I was fortunate to discuss Story with Kim Hudson and her studies have had a profound effect on Three Story Method. Below is a bit about Hudson and a transcript of my conversation with her.

Kim Hudson is a narrative theorist and a pioneer in storytelling from the feminine perspective. She's the originator of the 'Virgin' story structure. While a film student in Vancouver, Kim was told that all story from all time was based on one story, the Hero's Journey, one universal story.

Kim instantly recognized the power of the Hero's journey and began a lifelong journey to adapt and innovate the Hero's journey into a revolutionary paradigm to enhance the storytelling and screenwriting journey from the feminine perspective.

For the next two decades, she was thrown into her own quest to bring this new journey to life. Exploring mythology, psychology (Jung), story structure, and hundreds of movies, Kim recognized a second story structure. She described it in her ground-breaking book, The Virgin's Promise: Writing Stories of Creative, Spiritual and Sexual Awakening.

Kim has an unusual background. She is trained in geological exploration and is a specialist in treaty negotiation with indigenous people. She is currently a Fellow with Simon Fraser University Centre for Dialogue and Director of the Two Ways of Knowing project. She presents her unique story class internationally. She currently lives in the Yukon, Canada, with her daughters and her dog.

J.: Most of your research has been done for screenplays, and so I'm wondering if there are either subtle or major differences between how you would approach this for a novel versus a screenplay?

Kim: I would say the biggest difference is that in a novel, you just have so much more room. You can do so much with the interplay of your characters. So, that would be the biggest difference. And you have more time. You also have a lot more intimacy, like you're in the reader's head and you're also in the head of your characters, which means that a virgin's journey is way better for really engaging your audience because, in a hero's story, everything has an external focus.

You're asking, "Am I afraid or not?" But you really are shutting off your emotions to get the job done. Whereas, in a virgin story, it's all about exploring those feelings.

And, of course, in a novel, that's where you can really do that. So, a novel might actually be a better place for a virgin story. In the three-act structure, there are these natural crossovers between the two of them. And you have a lot more room in a novel, you could play with both characters. In other words, you could play with how a hero and a virgin are interacting. And there are natural crossovers.

J.: So, the ratio of the three-act structure is somewhat fluid between the two, but the sequencing for the virgin and the hero are really important for the reasons you've just mentioned.

Kim: No. I thought that when I wrote the book, but I would no longer say that.

The hero's is linear. The hero does have to go from 1 to 12, or it wouldn't make sense otherwise. But the virgin, she can do them in any order. Absolutely any order. You could start with her being rescued, and yet it means nothing because the change didn't happen inside.

J.: Are there certain beats that you find are more important or less important and why would that be the case?

Kim: I would say that all 13 beats are inherent to a believable transformation. And that's what virgin stories really are, internal transformation.

Now, having said that, some can be virtual, some can be that you recognize it because she is behaving differently, and so something had to have happened, and we can believe that that would have happened based on all the things that have gone before.

I would say every beat is important. Some can be assumed, some can be very brief. Body language says enormous things. But I would also say that there are three beats, but because we're so ingrained in the hero's journey that we often miss them. And I find this in my workshops a lot, that people are suddenly rolling along, and they just skip through all the moments of internal transformation.

Creating a secret world is basically saying, "I matter. What I want and my place in the world matters to me, and that's enough." That's a huge thing in this personal transformation. I would say that aspect of it, it's not being cowardly, it's not being tricky. It's basically saying, "If I want it, that is enough. I don't need anybody's approval to do it. I want it, and therefore, it's important."

Then the second one is beat six, which is "no longer fits her world." And the reason the secret world is secret is that before you're connected to yourself, you can't weather the storm of people planting seeds of doubt, or making you busy, or encouraging you to go back to your helpful roles. You need to have your own space and not be knocked down while you're still just a little seedling trying to grow up. But there will come a time when you're still in that space, but you're uncomfortable because you have gotten bigger in your connection to yourself and you start to make mistakes, or grumble, or let it drift from one world to the other, secret to dependent. That's important. So, "no longer fits her world" is the sign that you're ready to give up the secret world and introduce yourself to the dominant world and cause all the chaos that's gonna happen.

And then, the really big one is eight. And this gets missed all the time, "that it gives up what kept you stuck." And the point is that a long time ago, way back in beat two, "the price of conformity," you adopted a belief that was good for you. It may not seem like it now that you know who you are and what you can do, but you were making yourself small, and you were being super helpful, believing someday people are gonna turn around and say, "Okay, it's your turn. We'll help you now." Which of course never happens. But the point is that it probably helped you go along to get along when you had no power, or it gave you someplace to fit in even though it wasn't true belonging. At the time, for the power that you had, that was the best thing that you believed you could do. So, until you know yourself better, until you know more power, until you have more options, you keep doing that.

The difference is, beat eight, is where you have experienced a different sense of yourself, and now you can afford to go back and cut that umbilical cord and risk whether or not there is still a place of belonging for you because you have a place of belonging in yourself. If you cut that cord before you're connected to yourself, depression, anxiety, suicide— these are the things that happen because that existential crisis of not knowing who you are, believing you are valued and then being rejected is unbelievably painful. So, beat eight gets skipped over and must not.

J.: Given that this is a nonlinear story archetype, it seems like the creative palette is unlimited.

Kim: Absolutely. That access to your inner world in a novel is sheer magic.

J.: If you are a creative, whether it's a filmmaker or a novelist and your goal is to write a story for the ages—would you recommend writing a myth or a fairy tale?

Kim: The time is now for the fairy tale. The modernized fairy tale. We don't need to be in Renaissance clothing, but it has never been safer to live, especially in North America. We don't need to fight for our food or shelter most of the time.

The hero stories are not as relevant.

What we care about is how do we know what our place is going be? What's my true talent and how will I bring that to the world? How do I navigate social media when there could be huge forces that are telling me that I'm of no value and getting into me in a very personal way and I have to battle that even though the whole globe knows something about me? That's a big challenge to connect to yourself despite what everybody else thinks of you. Depression, anxiety, feeling disconnected from your community, the issues of being an immigrant and translocated—those are virgin stories. How do I know that I'm of value in whatever environment I find myself in?

Now that we don't have to fear so much and struggle for life, we expect life to be meaningful. And this is where a meaningful life is found. The more you connect to yourself, the more ability you have to listen, truly listen to other people because you know that your opinion is yours so you can afford to hear opinions that aren't yours and still filter whether or not you're going to make it yours. There's that agency.

You have the generosity when you know what's meant for you to offer to others, what's not meant for you and that builds strong relationships, and better communities and these types of journeys are the stories of our age. A writer who tells stories this way will have a legacy.

J.: It's been 10 years since you published the book. Looking at the social landscape these days and what's been changing for people who have been suppressed or marginalized— especially women, if you were going to update *The Virgin's*

Promise or write a new introduction, what might you add, or change?

Kim: I wished I'd had been more intentional about masculine/feminine as opposed to male/female. This is not a story just for women. And I think that some of the best stories are men exploring their feminine side. We expect more from the man, like in *About a Boy* or *The Shape of Water*.

I would really explore the meaning of power and the differences between a hero's power and a virgin's power.

Linear, or hero power, is to assert your will even against the will of others, which is basically like a hero fighting evil. If you don't take enough action, then you're in the coward archetypical zone, or you're frozen like a deer in the headlights. And if you do too much, you're the tyrant. You're creating collateral damage, do anything to win. You're always looking for a sweet spot in the middle. And that's what makes a hero and it will also make the more mature masculine, which is the warrior king or even a mentor. They're always trying to find that middle zone.

I came up with the idea of circular power or feminine power, virgin power is basically to know yourself, to be yourself, take action on that, and to support others in doing the same. And it's extremely empowering, it's extremely connecting to who you are and probably one of the most powerful things you can do if you're trying to be happy or authentic. It's an equally viable form of power and arguably, more relevant now.

There is no good or evil in any feminine power. And there's no such thing as knowing yourself too well or supporting others too much. The qualifier is that the feelings that you focus on will grow and be contagious. If you focus on disconnected feelings, then you feel disconnected to your-self, and you will generate disconnection in the people around you and in your own life. But if you focus on your own feelings of connection, that will grow, and it will be like a drop of water, and more and more people will have that sense of, "I, too, can find my place in the world, and my sense of connection and I can afford to be vulnerable."

The biggest challenge for me has been the word virgin. I spent my whole life defining virgin, like a virgin forest, meaning your value just for being yourself before anybody can get their hackles up and go, "Oh my God, the virgin victim thing again." I fight with that. But I have come to recognize that that is the crux of it. We are not a culture that understands the victim to virgin journey, and we have pushed back against it.

There are two understandings of what it means to be a victim. There's a masculine and a feminine understanding. In the masculine understanding, a victim is somebody who has been wronged. It's a call to their heroic. And the bigger that person, the wrongdoing towards that person, the greater the hero is. And the more sustained that person's victimhood is, the more they can rally the troops. If a person recovers, the energy of the fight is lost. So, if a person wants to perpetuate linear masculine power, they need to stay victimized. And it's detrimental to the victim. It's great for heroic energy, but not so good for the victim.

In feminine energy, the victim is a moment of awakening. It's the recognition when you have been through an experi-ence, and you take the time to look inward and notice, "What has been my assessment of that and how has that shaped my sense of myself? Have I internalized the belief that I was of low value, that society doesn't care about me, that maybe I deserved it in some way?" And that moment is when you have made a connection to what you truly feel and you've moved from the shadow side of victimhood, which is being disconnected from the positive side, which is knowing that you have a journey to take between being disconnected and becoming reconnected to your value. That is empowering—only you can decide what you believe about yourself. And that's why you start the 13 steps of the virgin's story.

I would even argue that the women's movement has chosen a heroic path. We're always fighting back against the places where we're excluded and rather than embracing the feminine and feminine ways of doing things—to embrace the personal storytelling, letting ourselves shine and reconnect so that people can see what it would look like when we contribute our authentic thoughts.

Don't always push back, instead, pull in what you want more. Try and make a connection and then see where it can grow from there as opposed to calling them out, pushing them back because people don't grow in that environment. They learn to go underground, they learn to not speak.

J.: The mono-myth is so ingrained. It's probably not surprising that it has become a default for many people in many situations.

Kim: And I've done it, too. It's not a judgment. But now that I know the two options, I make a choice more often.

CASE STUDY – SCI-FI SEATTLE SHORT STORY, "TEMPLE OF THE DOGS"

In the fall of 2019, we hosted an event in Washington called "Sci-Fi Seattle." Below is the final version of that short story. At the retreat, we used Three Story Method to plan and then write it. You can download the worksheet for "Temple of the Dogs" by going here: https://thecareerauthor.com/3smlinksandresources/

"Temple of the Dogs" by Zach Bohannon and J. Thorn

LAYNE KNEW the Teku would eventually call his number, but he never imagined he'd be leaving alone.

His communicator squawked, informing him that it was time to move to C-Deck. The scratchy, robotic voice told him to take nothing, and to proceed immediately.

The residents living on the Teku ship *Sona* knew what that meant.

As he slid shut the scuffed, steel door to his living quarters, Layne muted the navigation bot dictating directions through the communicator clipped to his ear. He worked as a maintenance engineer on *Sona* for years—he was as familiar with every crack in her hull as he was with the thin veins crawling across the back of his hands.

Layne ran his fingers through a long, black beard, his green eyes darting back and forth from beneath shaggy bangs. The scar under his right eye twitched as he thought about what would happen on C-Deck today, the one *Sona's* passengers called Cleansing Day.

Several others passed Layne as he stood in the tubular hallway outside of his room. They all focused on the tops of their gravity boots, shuffling along without speaking.

How long had it been since the Teku had taken their colony captive? Five years? Ten years? Time on the ship smeared like a far-flung nebula, burning out and burning cold. Their alien overlords promised not to break apart families, but worry always consumed Alisha. She didn't believe that the Teku commanders would keep their word, that their family would be split up once the *Sona* jettisoned the pods.

He remembered debating the biobatts with his wife. Alisha thought hers would deplete first, but Layne insisted that his would, given that he had more biomass than her. In the end, it didn't matter. Layne was leaving *Sona* today. Alone.

"C'mon, sir. Proceed to C-Deck."

He looked up to see who had spoken. A woman. But not just any woman. Layne would never forget her eyes, the ones that apologized to him when both Alisha and their baby died in childbirth. In *this* doctor's medic tube.

Layne didn't think she recognized him. She delivered all of the pregnancies on *Sona,* and many ended in tragedy, thanks to the radiation pummeling the ship during deep space travel. His wife and child weren't the first to die during childbirth, but this doctor *should* have remembered him. She had to know who he was.

"I know the way," he said, but the doctor had already turned the corner, and another group of tagged residents made their way toward C-Deck.

Alisha wouldn't have wanted him to give up, to accept a death sentence from the random and routine banishment enforced by the Teku. But he found it difficult to care about much since her passing.

A man and a woman stood in front of Layne as he approached the elevator. Neither had punched the button, so he pushed between them, slapping the cold aluminum button with the meat of his right fist, grunting as if the movement caused him pain. Neither said a word to Layne and he didn't look at them again.

After what felt like hours, the elevator arrived. The steel doors slid open soundlessly, and a puff of oxygen filled the cabin—the Teku believed the pure element would help calm the frantic humans as they marched to their own galactic ostracism. It seemed to work. The man looked up and smiled briefly at Layne.

The door shut and the car descended so quickly that Layne's stomach flipped. And then, empty of food for at least the past 16 hours, it grumbled. When the elevator stopped at C-Deck, the doors opened, and he followed the man and woman into a narrow hallway with no doors. Tubes and

cables ran the length of the hallway, connecting to an appa-
ratus that resembled the steel skeleton of a long-forgotten
mutant race.

"Please stand by for full-body scan," the machine said
through his communicator.

The robot's arms wrapped around Layne, blue lights in its
fingers, scanning his entire body. After several moments, a
green light flashed on the machine's monitor, alerting the
Teku guard that Layne had passed the scan. He didn't
understand why the Teku would care what they had with
them once they jettisoned from *Sona*. But rules were rules
and the Teku followed theirs as blindly as humans had done
in their past.

"No forbidden objects detected," the robot said, this time
through the small speaker mounted in its side. "Please walk
to pod number nine."

The door behind the robot scanner opened. Layne stepped
around the machine and through the doorway.

Transport pods lined each side of the room, reaching thirty
or forty feet into the deepening darkness at the other end of
the pod bay. Several humans sat inside, staring through the
port view on the main hatch and waiting for the ejection
phase.

He counted seven, eight, and then turned right to face an
open pod with a number 9 hastily painted above the bay.
Layne took a step to the side, listening as others walked past
his pod to their own.

The Teku claimed to be seeding the universe with human

settlements. They told those aboard *Sona* that the ship periodically reached maximum capacity, which then triggered a Cleansing Day.

"A New Beginning," was how the Teku talked about those shot from *Sona* to the unforgiving surface of some barren planet. The phrase was only half-true.

The suit waited for him as he turned around and lowered his body into the pod. Layne heard a whir and then a click as the suit activated, slithering over his body according to the custom dimensions from his last scan. Layne thought the suit was silly—a way for the Teku to absolve themselves of the guilt. Sure, they would eject people like space trash, but they also gave them a form-fitting bio-suit that could serve as a burial shroud.

Layne didn't know the odds, didn't know how many people survived Cleansing Day. He didn't care.

The Teku promised a suit with enough oxygen to make it to the hive, and some did. But others told him stories of previous ejections on Cleansing Day, ones when no communicators pinged a reply from the planet's surface.

He sat back as the hatch slid into place, the seals creating a bubble of safe air that would be enough to get him to the surface before his suit started supplying oxygen. Layne now stared out through his viewport at the others marching to their pods, just as those in the other pods had done.

The couple from the elevator walked by, the woman crying as she let go of her husband's hand and climbed into her own pod.

At least they know the odds, he thought as he closed his eyes. They understand the risks, and that many people die on Cleansing Day.

He thought of Alisha, with her long, dark hair pulled back, and her face sweaty as she pushed through the contractions. She hadn't received a pod. Neither had their son. His family's odds had been zero on that day, which was what he felt like inside. Layne recalled the blood pooling beneath his wife's delivery table, the lifeless newborn in the midwife bot's arms.

His eyes shot open, and he gasped.

"Heart rate—rapid increase. Calming sequence initiated."

"I'm fine," Layne said aloud to the AI voice in his communicator. "What's it matter, anyway? In a few minutes, we won't be your problem anymore."

"Launch sequence initiated," came the reply, the AI no longer concerned about Layne's heart rate. "Recline and strap in."

Do I have a choice?

The safety restraints came over his shoulders and snaked around his waist, securing him to the pod's seat. The blinking lights inside the craft dimmed as the nav system booted on a glowing display at eye level, which now obstructed his line of sight through the viewport. Of course, it did. The Teku avoided last-minute human freak-outs by not letting them see what was about to happen.

"Coordinates identified." A new AI voice came through the communicator, most likely version 1.6 of the MOMA Protocol. "Godspeed, sir."

Layne chuckled, remembering the clunky language of that version before they patched it with a more human-like cadence. "Thanks a lot, asshole."

"Finalizing launch sequence."

He swallowed, his hands sweating, and his legs shaking as the timer counted down toward zero. When the counter hit 1, Layne closed his eyes and clenched his mouth shut as the pod ejected from the bay with so much force that Layne believed the safety restraints would cut him in half.

He gasped as the g-force pushed his heart into his stomach. Layne opened his eyes, but darkness collapsed his vision as if he was staring down a darkened tunnel with a dim light at the end. The pod spun end over end. He watched the alternating void of space and the bright orange aura of Planet CC-2017 as he rolled, torpedoing toward the bare surface.

The g-force on his body lessened as the pod's rotation slowed. He raised his head and looked out through the side viewport which was blocked back in the bay.

Space lorded over him, a black velvet sea of eternity. A few renegade stars blinked in the distance. And then the nose of the pod turned and angled toward the planet's surface as gravity pulled him toward the amber oceans of sand below.

Layne reached out and put his gloved hand on the pod's inner wall, feeling the heat from atmospheric entry threatening to melt the thin metal—the only thing separating him from instant annihilation.

After years spent on *Sona* and traversing endless galaxies, Layne couldn't have prepared for a voyage like this. The adrenaline surged through his system, and his mouth turned up at the corners. A slight chuckle fell from his lips as he thought about how much Alisha would have enjoyed the free fall.

He turned from the viewport to the monitor, checking his elevation and estimated landing coordinates.

A black screen stared back.

"What the hell?"

And then the pod's engine shut down.

Layne blinked. "Navigation, on."

Nothing.

"Navigation, on!" he screamed.

Still nothing.

Layne tapped on the monitor. Grinding his teeth, he slammed his fist against the black screen.

"Come on, you son of a bitch. Work!"

Gravity never malfunctioned. It worked the same in every corner of the universe. The pod's navigation system failed, but the planet's gravitational pull would guide it to the surface, although not at the speed or with the destination coordinates the Teku programmed for pod number nine.

Layne's gloved hand shook as he reached for the emergency inflation device. He knew about the early space travelers and how they would use inflated plastic to lessen the landing impact on a planet without much gravity. Whether the Teku had stolen that technology or invented their own didn't matter—it was the only fail-safe built into the pods.

As the pod sliced through the upper levels of the atmosphere, the air currents knocked it around like a leaf in a hurricane.

Layne gripped the armrests and closed his eyes as the surface rushed up to greet him. As an engineer, he knew how fast the pod was traveling and what would happen if the emergency inflation device failed—in a split second, his body would be vaporized. But at least Layne would be reunited with Alisha and their stillborn son.

The pod flipped, and something came loose and struck Layne's helmet, ringing it like a bell. His eyes fluttered and he heard the ungodly sound of air tearing at the pod's thin skin.

He moaned and felt the bile rise in his throat as smoke began to fill the pod.

I'm coming home to you, love.

Layne closed his eyes, and everything went black.

SMOKE FILLED THE SPACE, and Layne awoke to the sensation of heat coming from beneath his seat.

Where am I? What is going on?

He blinked and held up a hand, rotating it around. Display lights flickered, and a low hum pulsed in his communicator.

"I'm alive," he said to convince himself.

Manually unbuckling the restraints, Layne leaned forward

to look at the pod's monitor. His head began to ache, and he felt a sharp stab in his side as he took a deep breath. Otherwise, Layne survived the crash landing unscathed—a miracle he didn't appreciate. He could have been with Alisha. He should be with her now.

He tapped the screen several times, but whatever caused the malfunction during the descent was still preventing the system from booting. Layne rattled off as many AI commands as he could remember, but did not receive an answer. The dead communicator sat on his ear like a pesky fly.

After ensuring the landing hadn't punctured his suit, Layne whacked the manual release on the hatch. He swung his legs over the side of the smoking pod and planted his boots on the ground. Alisha would have loved this. They had dreamed of visiting a planet someday, though both of them living their entire lives aboard *Sona*.

He walked around the pod, realizing the aliens running the ship kept the gravity force about the same as most habitable planets in the Belltwin System. Layne heard the crunch of the rocky, orange soil beneath his feet, along with the whistling of wind that blew smoke from the pod off into the distance. Even through the air filtration unit in his suit, he could taste the foreign grains of sand in his mouth.

Spinning around in a complete circle, Layne looked to the horizon in every direction. He saw nothing but one massive boulder about 4 bitclicks to the south.

"Great. Just great."

He checked the transponder on his wrist. The Teku had

placed a holographic pin on the hive's coordinates. The pod was supposed to land him within 10 bitclicks of the place. He should've been able to identify it from his landing site.

He didn't.

To the north, the land swelled up to a ridge. Layne jogged toward the ridge's summit, his right side burning with every breath. He would need to visit the medic at the hive to get his ribs wrapped.

Layne stood on the top of the ridge, peering down into the valley below. He saw nothing but the desolate land—more sand, dirt, and rocks.

Dropping down to his knees, Layne glanced again at his wrist transponder. Then he fired another batch of commands at the AI.

Silence.

"Think, Layne."

No food. No water. No way of knowing where he was or how far the hive was from his current location.

What else do I need but don't have?

Layne shook his head.

"Oxygen."

The planet's atmosphere didn't support life, which didn't matter if you were inside of the hive. Not only was he outside of it, but he didn't know where his pod landed. Layne might be 15 bitclicks away, or 15 teraclicks away. Regardless of the distance to traverse, each suit on *Sona* was equipped with two tanks—about three hours' worth of oxygen. In theory, that would be enough to cover the humans from the pod landing site to the hive. In reality, he already burned at least 20 minutes of his supply.

Layne spun around several times as he scanned the land-scape. His heart rate accelerated, and he took a few deep breaths.

Calm down. If you lose your shit, you're going to run out of oxygen even faster, and you're never going to make it to the hive.

"Hello!"

At first, Layne thought the voice came from inside of his head, but it came from his communicator—the AI voice replaced by a human one, a strange juxtaposition on the lifeless surface of CC-2017.

"Can you hear me through your communicator?"

He turned around in time to see a woman walking toward him, wearing a *Sona* pod suit and waving both arms.

"Yes, I think so." Layne blinked and shook his head, hoping the crash landing hadn't scrambled his brains.

"I need your help."

Something about her voice startled him. He stopped, waiting for her to approach through the worsening dust storm. She stepped through the dirty cloud like a ghost.

"Are you injured?"

Layne swiped a gloved hand across his face shield and blinked a few times to focus his vision. It couldn't be.

"It's you," he said as she stopped a few feet away. "You ruined my life."

"Excuse me?"

"You're responsible for the death of my wife and son."

The woman stared at Layne as his eyes filled with tears.

"Sir, I don't know you. I was on—"

"Shut up. If I'm going to die on this godforsaken planet, the last thing I want is your voice in my communicator. Leave me alone."

Layne turned his back on her, but he heard his communicator crackle, which preceded the sound passing through the suit's external mic and into his listening device.

"I'm Dr. Riley Price. I'm the—"

"I know who you are. My wife *and* my son died in your hands."

"Oh my God..."

Layne spun around to see Price about five feet away, both of her gloved hands held up in front of her face shield.

"I'm so sorry. Your wife, her name was—"

"Alisha. Her name was Alisha."

"You must understand. Every childbirth is a risky procedure. Sometimes things are beyond our control."

"Oh, yes, Doctor," Layne almost spat sarcasm on the inside of his face shield. "Like the Teku. They don't care about us, and you do their bidding. I'm sure my son was just another human unit to you and them, but he was *my* son. He's gone and so is my beautiful wife."

Dr. Price shook her head, tears streaming down her face. "It's not like that. I took the Hippocratic Oath. I value every human life, from every deck of *Sona*."

Layne waved a hand at her. "I don't care. We've both crash-landed hundreds or thousands of bitclicks from the hive. Please leave me alone and let me die in peace."

"Please, wait."

He turned his back to Price and stomped off toward what he perceived was the western horizon. A few more bitclicks and his communicator would be out of range of hers.

"I have a child with me."

Layne stopped. He closed his eyes and took a deep breath, staring at the ragged, orange horizon. "What?"

"Not mine, but a child of *Sona*. I've been treating her for a rare blood disorder. The Teku sent me here with her. The girl's number came up, and so, I volunteered to go with her on Cleansing Day. If I can get to the diagnostic computers at the hive, I might be able to cure her."

He turned and noticed that Price had walked closer but still kept a bitclick between them.

"Not my problem."

"She's a child." The doctor shook her head inside the helmet. "She needs your help."

"In case you haven't noticed, we've got a few hours of oxygen and broken transponders. None of this will matter soon."

Price shook her head. "What do you mean?"

"I mean, we don't have a clue where we are. How do you expect to find the hive?"

She held up her arm and pulled down the cuff of the suit to expose her transponder, which was lit and flashing. "Mine works."

He sighed, and the pain in his ribs reminded him of life. It was brutal and painful, but we all held onto it for as long as we could.

"How far?"

"Forty, maybe fifty bitclicks from here."

Layne did the math in his head. If they started walking right now, they just might make it before using up the rest of the oxygen.

"Forget about me." Price was now an arm's length from Layne. "Help the girl. Help us to the hive, and then, we'll take things from there."

He stood up straight despite the pain in his ribs. "Take me to the girl."

THEY TRUDGED a few bitclicks across the sandy terrain to where Dr. Price's pod rested in a heaping pile of metal. Layne noted the number of her pod—49-2—one of the few designed to carry multiple humans.

As they approached and Price led him around the side of the pod, Layne saw the girl for the first time. She sat on the ground, her knees awkwardly up to her chin in a suit that appeared to be two sizes too large.

He walked to the girl before squatting down in front of her.

"What's your name, sweetie?"

The girl didn't answer.

"She's still in shock, and we're wasting time."

"If you want my help, shut up." Layne looked over his shoulder at Price, who nodded, her top teeth biting into her bottom lip.

"What's your name?"

"Tanya."

"Hi, Tanya. I'm Layne. I'm here to make sure you arrive at the hive, okay?"

"Okay."

"How old are you?"

"Seven."

"That's exactly what I was going to guess."

The girl smiled, which brought one to Layne's face.

"Now, listen," Layne said. "I know that the crash was scary. I had one, too. It wasn't any fun. But we're going to get to the hive, all right?"

The girl nodded.

"Can you walk?"

"I think so."

Layne stood and then offered his hand to the girl. She took it, and he pulled her up to her feet. Tanya wobbled on her boots but then seemed to stabilize on the sand, a sensation not experienced on the stainless steel floors of *Sona*.

He turned to Price. "Which way?"

"West," Price answered, but she didn't tell Layne the coordinates or offer him her transponder.

Layne took Tanya by the hand. "Then let's go."

He didn't know how much oxygen Price or Tanya had left. And besides, Layne doubted the suit would be able to protect them from the brutal temperatures that would grip the planet's surface once the sun set.

"Are we almost there?" Tanya asked.

"Yeah, hon. Almost."

He didn't lie. They were almost *somewhere*.

THE WIND WHIPPED off the distant mesa bringing cyclonic columns of dust and dirt that pelted Layne's face shield. He leaned forward to keep the gusts from getting underneath his body and blowing him over on to his back. CC-2017's lonely, cold sun dropped closer to the horizon, and he could see ice crystals forming on the ends of his gloves.

Tanya walked behind Layne, taking advantage of the laws of

aerodynamics. Price stumbled along behind the girl, making sure she didn't fall too far behind Layne.

He estimated they walked for an hour, but given the rapidly deteriorating weather, it was difficult to know if they were making progress. Price didn't give him updates from her transponder, and Layne didn't want them. Finding out they'd only covered five or six bitclicks would be too demoralizing.

"She needs a rest."

He rolled his eyes as the doctor's comment came through his communicator. Layne shook his head.

"Can't. Temperature is dropping, and the Teku didn't design our suits for it. If we don't get to the hive before nightfall, we'll freeze to death out here."

He winced, realizing that Tanya's communicator was on their shared frequency. But their situation was dire, and lying to the girl or dumbing it down for her wouldn't be fair. If Tanya was going to survive in this new world, she would need to understand life's harsh realities. It would have been what he taught his own son.

"Stop!"

Price's voice was broken glass coming through his communicator.

Layne stopped and spun. "I said, I don't think—"

Tanya had dropped to her knees, her head down so that Layne saw his reflection in the top of her helmet—his face ashen, distorted.

"Are you all right?" he asked Tanya.

"Her condition causes her to tire easily. I'm afraid if we don't let her rest that she might not be able to walk much farther."

Layne thought about the oxygen in his suit, and then about the same biosystems running in theirs. Price didn't mention it, but she could read the same readouts as he could—not only were they running out of daylight, they were running out of oxygen as well.

"I'll carry her." The increased exertion would tax his oxygen supply, but he'd rather risk his life trying than collapsing into the orange sands and letting this planet take it.

"We still have another—"

"Don't tell me how far away we are." Layne took a deep breath, wondering how many more of those he could spare. "I really don't want to know."

Tanya stood and looked at him. She smiled, but she did so through bloodshot eyes and sunken cheeks.

"Hop on, kid."

He turned around and squatted in front of Tanya, letting her wrap her arms around the tanks on his back. He hitched up, reaching back and putting his hands beneath the bottom of her suit to create a saddle.

Tanya giggled through his communicator. "Giddyup!"

ONE FOOT in front of the other. He kept walking, no longer thinking about the Teku or his life aboard *Sona*. Even memories of Alisha slid to the back of his mind as the physical demands increased on his body. Before, he believed he would see his wife and son again in the afterlife. But every painful step made that seem like an impossible dream.

The sharp pain in his ribs had turned from a butter knife to a chain saw. His head throbbed, and he swore he could taste the sand in his mouth and feel it in his throat. At first, he barely noticed Tanya's weight on his back. But bitclick after bitclick, she turned into a hunk of heavy metal.

The sun dropped to within a few degrees of the horizon and his oxygen gauge fell into the red zone.

"I think I can walk for a little bit."

"Okay." He didn't ask her twice, allowing the girl to slide off his back.

"Do you need a moment?" Dr. Price asked.

Layne shook his head. "We need to keep going."

They resumed the single-file march, a funerary procession of three.

"Thank you for carrying her. We wouldn't have made it this far without you."

Now he wanted to know how many bitclicks there were to go before reaching the hive. But he didn't ask Price. He couldn't force his mouth to form the words. Instead, he responded, "Just trying to save the kid."

Price nodded even though he couldn't see her face. "I know you don't want to hear this, but I'm sorry for your loss."

"You're right. I don't want to hear it."

"Well, you're going to hear some of it anyway, unless you have some way of ripping your communicator off your ear."

Layne considered it for a moment, but removing his helmet would mean certain death. He didn't know what would kill him first—the cold, the lack of oxygen, or this woman's lame-ass excuses.

"I had to make a choice, Layne, and I chose to try and save your wife. I failed, and if you don't think I'm haunted by what happened in that medic tube every day of my life, then..."

He listened. Her tone shifted, not accusatory but sad, and Layne preferred her to be combative, so he wouldn't have to think about how difficult of a decision that must have been for her. He said nothing, allowing her to continue as they trudged along.

"You don't have to forgive me. But I want you to know that I tried. I did the best I could. I swear to God."

"Look!"

Layne turned to see Tanya pointing at three hazy shapes about a bitclick deep in the growing darkness. The winds died down as if suffocated by the dropping temperature.

"What is it?" Layne asked.

"Pods. Jettisoned," Dr. Price answered.

He felt the answer in her voice, which meant he had to ask. "How far are we from the hive?"

"At least two hours, maybe more."

Layne didn't need to do the math. He knew. If they combined tanks, two of them would have enough oxygen to make it there. But not three.

"What's it called?" he asked Price. "Every hive has a nickname."

"Temple of the Dogs."

"Why do they call it that?" Tanya asked.

Layne also wanted to know, but Price could only guess.

"I heard that the first settlers arrived with dogs, and the dogs had to be sacrificed to keep the humans alive." Price sighed. "But that's legend. You'll have to ask the people living there when we arrive."

HE SMILED as he swore he saw Alisha sitting next to Tanya in the sand, and he noticed reflections of his son on the girl's face—a family outing that would never be.

"I have something for you both."

Price saw Layne's hands go to the valves on both of his oxygen tanks. He turned them off, giving him about 15 minutes' worth still circulating through his suit.

"What are you doing?"

It was Alisha's voice he heard through his communicator, but Dr. Price stood before him, her eyes wide and mouth agape.

"It still might not be enough oxygen, but it'll at least give you both a shot of getting there. But don't stop again. The cold will put you to sleep, and you'll never wake up."

He held out the tanks to her, eyebrows raised. "Take them. No point in all three of us dying."

"But, Layne. I can't leave you here."

"Get her to the hive, Price. And get yourself there, too. There are humans to save, and they'll need qualified doctors to keep the colony alive. Doctors who try their best, even if they don't always save the patient."

She grimaced and then a smile momentarily flashed on her face. "Aren't you coming with us?"

Layne stooped down and looked into the girl's eyes. "The doc here is going to take you the rest of the way. She cares about you. She'll get you to the hive and save your life. I just know it."

"But what will happen to you?"

"I'm going to take a nap and then decide what to do." At least he wasn't lying to the kid.

Price attached one tank to Tanya's back and hooked the other on her belt. She stared at Layne, tears streaming down her face.

"I'm sorry."

"Don't be sorry. Be strong. Find the Temple of the Dogs."

He stood and watched as Price led the girl by the hand into the darkness. Layne sat down on a rock, dizzy and with dark circles crawling in from the edge of his vision.

The sand turned into a lush, green field of tall grass, and Layne saw Alisha walking toward him, her dark hair braided, her skin glowing beneath a white sundress. By her side walked a boy of about five, smiling at him with Alisha's bright eyes.

Alisha reached out, extending her hand to Layne. "Come home to us."

"I'm on my way, love."

Layne sat back with a smile on his face as he closed his eyes.

The End.

USING TAROT WITH CAROLINE DONAHUE

Another interesting spin on the Hero's Journey archetype can be found by authors such as Caroline Donahue. Her book, *Story Arcana*, is a short guide designed to illustrate how authors can use tarot cards to craft a story and I'd highly recommend it if you want to learn more. The Major Arcana of the tarot has been loosely mapped to Campbell's stages of the Hero's Journey.

ABOUT CAROLINE (FROM HER WEBSITE):

As a book-loving Writing and Book Coach, I don't believe there is any force more powerful in this world than writing. The more of us who speak up through our writing, the better. As our world becomes more complex, we need to read more books from more perspectives. Let's get your book written together.

WITH A MASTERS in Psychology and Expressive Arts, and a subsequent career in the book world that began with working in a bookshop, progressing through editing and producing a thrice annual auction catalogue, to proofreading for a prominent ad agency, I have apprenticed myself to writing for over ten years. In 2016, I launched The Secret Library Podcast and have since interviewed over 100 writers, editors, agents, and publishers to get to the bottom of what it takes to write a book. I'm currently writing my own novel and co-editing the anthology, I Wrote it Anyway.

I'VE MAPPED the Major Arcana stages to Luke's journey in *Star Wars: A New Hope*. Donahue helped me to clarify the interpretations.

DEPARTURE

Home or Ordinary World – Fool Stage

Luke is a typical teenager, living with his uncle and aunt on the planet Tatooine. He helps them manage the farm and often complains about doing his chores, an ordinary world like any other. But he also shows signs of being discontent when his uncle refuses to let Luke apply to the academy until the following year.

THE CALL TO ADVENTURE, Awakening – Magician and High Priestess Stage

"Help me Obi-Wan Kenobi. You're my only hope." After seeing Princess Leia's hologram projected from a message inside of R2-D2, Luke is enamored with her and the struggle that is happening at the galactic level. He's intrigued and wants to know more and although it's not clear at the time, it will be a call he cannot ultimately refuse.

REFUSAL OF THE CALL – Empress and Emperor

Old Ben, as Obi-Wan is called before he is revealed to be the mentor, suggests to Luke that there might be more to this world than buying droids and helping his Uncle Owen on the farm. But Luke isn't interested yet, tragically believing the situation out there will never ripple back to him on the desolate planet of Tatooine. He has his chores to finish and he's concerned about what will happen if he doesn't attend to them.

SUPERNATURAL AID/MENTOR – Hierophant

Old Ben emerges as the mentor Obi-Wan Kenobi, a Jedi warrior who fought in the Clone Wars with Luke's father. Obi-Wan saves Luke after an ambush from the Sand People. He offers to teach Luke the ways of the Force, like his father, but Luke again refuses the call. Meeting the Mentor transitions into Crossing the Threshold when Luke returns to the farm to discover his uncle and aunt have been murdered. He says to Obi-Wan, "There's nothing for me here now. I want to learn the ways of the Force and become a Jedi like my father."

DARTH VADER COULD ALSO BE SEEN as the hierophant, a figure representing the oppressive cultural norms that Luke will be forced to confront.

. . .

CROSSING THE FIRST THRESHOLD – **Lovers**

The threshold for Luke is his journey to the Mos Eisley spaceport where he has now left his old life behind. He is clearly uncomfortable in the Cantina, akin to a country boy walking the big city streets for the first time. Obi-Wan guides and protects Luke, as a good mentor should.

PRINCESS LEIA, in an understated way, has become an obsession of Luke's, going back to the first time he sees her in R2-D2's projection. But Luke is uncomfortable with his infatuation with Leia, who we later discover is his sister.

THE BELLY OF THE WHALE, **Chariot or Innermost Cave – Hermit**

On the Millennium Falcon, Obi-Wan Kenobi begins Luke's Jedi training in preparation for the inevitable conflict. They practice lightsaber moves, and Kenobi teaches him more about the Force. But Alderaan is gone and in its place is the Death Star, which will represent Luke's innermost cave. He looks at the massive ship and begins to doubt himself and his abilities.

INITIATION

Tests Stage – Strength

Luke discovers that Princess Leia has been captured by Darth Vader and he is holding her hostage in the Death Star. His strength, both physical and mental, will be tested.

. . .

Chewbacca also represents strength in the Tests Stage, a massive, "crazy" beast but also a helpful ally of Luke.

Preparation, Allies and Enemies Stage – Hermit

Trying to convince Han Solo and Chewbacca to help him isn't easy, but Luke must do so to discover his allies and his enemies. He is the lone voice of the crew, the "hermit" who is advocating for a course of action that he isn't entirely sure will work.

Chewbacca is taken "hostage" by Skywalker and Solo wearing stormtrooper suits, which allows them to walk through the Death Star and into the prison block. Identities are fluid, and Luke is trying to discover who can be trusted.

Meeting with the Goddess Stage – Wheel of Fortune

Luke meets the "goddess," Leia, and helps to break her out of the prison block. They escape by following her down a garbage chute that Leia has created by firing a laser into the wall.

Guardian Threshold – Justice

Luke's mentor sacrifices himself, engaging and distracting Darth Vader but ultimately giving up his life so Luke can escape (after Obi-Wan has disabled the Death Star's tractor beam). The ordeal is the obstacle the hero must overcome which Luke demonstrates by finding and then rescuing Princess Leia.

ATONEMENT STAGE – Temperance

When Luke hears Obi-Wan's voice telling him to run immediately after being struck down by Darth Vader, Luke forgives his mentor for the self-sacrifice. He understands that his mission is greater than the life of one man and that he cannot fail.

APOTHEOSIS, The Gift Stage – Tower

Luke's "sword" is the fact that he's now a pilot for the rebels. Ironically, this is exactly what he'd wished for while arguing with his Uncle Owen back in the ordinary world. His foundation is torn away, a crumbling of the life he once knew, which propels him into a different place.

HE WILL NEED to wield this weapon to gain the reward of his journey, although against what appears to be insurmountable odds. But Luke is a teenager, full of ambition and a belief that he is invincible. Along with what he's learned about the Force from his mentor, Luke is positioned to fulfill his journey and take the Road Back.

RETURN

Rescue from Without Stage – The Star

As Luke is preparing to join the X-Wing Red Squadron, he is

rescued from without by two instances. Obi-Wan speaks to him again with a whisper, "The Force will be with you." And, he reunites with the "goddess" and the feminine side when Leia kisses Luke on the lips for good luck.

THE ROAD BACK, Flight Stage, The Moon – Shadow Archetype

For Luke, his only way back to an ordinary world is to rid this one of the Death Star. And to do so means he must join the other pilots in a suicide mission to attack a known vulnerability of the Death Star, although with a small chance of success. Princess Leia is leading the plan's execution, her feminine intuition strong in the shadow archetype.

RIGHT BEFORE THE CAMPAIGN BEGINS, Han Solo offers to take Luke with him as he's fleeing the Death Star, but Luke refuses because that road doesn't lead back to the ordinary world.

CROSSING THE FINAL THRESHOLD STAGE – The Sun

Most of his squadron is shot down, and it appears as though the Empire has successfully fought off the attack until Luke gets a little help from Han Solo, which allows him to make a final attack run in his X-Wing Fighter. Luke must "fly into the sun" as he prepares to bring down the Death Star against seemingly insurmountable odds. At this moment, Luke knows what must be done and therefore, his challenge is out in the light and his mood optimistic.

· · ·

Resurrection, Master of the Two World's Stage – Judgment

Although Luke doesn't physically die on the mission, he is reborn as a different person. Luke's "old self" dies as he pushes the technology aside and taps into the Force as Obi-Wan taught him. He places a perfect shot without his guidance system, destroying the Death Star. Luke is now in the early stages of his resurrection as a Jedi warrior.

The Elixir, Freedom Stage – The World

He doesn't physically return with the magic potion that will change things, but that is metaphorically represented in the medal ceremony presided over by Princess Leia. Luke doesn't return to Tatooine yet, but he has brought that freedom to others throughout the galaxy, showing that his actions mattered. Luke's legacy has been established as the story comes to an end of the cycle where the battle has been won, but the war is far from over.

USING RUNES WITH MARC GRAHAM

Marc Graham has an interesting methodology that he's developed from ancient runes. Below is a bit about Graham from his website and a transcript of my conversation with him.

I'm a novelist and explorer in the Source of Story. I believe all writers should be the heroes of their own creative journey. I want to help writers use the power of story to transform live.

I am about writing with purpose. It is important, of course, to entertain one's readers, but it's equally important that the person who closes the book is not the same one who opened it. The reader's mind should be stretched and expanded, their world should be a little bigger, their outlook a bit brighter.

Marc: I've been a student of different esoteric traditions and paths for many, many years, 20, 30 years probably. I'd grown up, most of my adulthood, believing that I was of Celtic origins. Graham is a Scottish clan. I've looked into Druidry and the different Celtic scripts. And then, did a little digging and found out I'm much more Norse-related. So, the Scottish side of the family came over with William the Conqueror from Normandy, which had initially been settled by the Norse. So, it kind of spurred my interest to get back into studying the runes and find my true tradition.

The runes have been used, similar to the tarot, for millennia, for thousands of years as a divinatory tool by the Norse shamans prior to them becoming an alphabet since they were largely illiterate until just a few hundred years ago. So, it was really more of a personal development exercise for me, and connecting to that history and that ancestry, and finding a new way of a personal and spiritual expression. I have a rune teacher who has been guiding me in this and helping me understand how they are used for personal development, how they are used to understand the flow of energy within your own life.

There are 24 runes in the Elder Futhark, one of the specific alphabets. So, I was taking one a week and using that as my focus in my meditation. And about halfway through, as I was singing my meditation, just like Athena from Zeus' forehead, I was like, "This is how you can use this for story."

I got the first idea with rune cards, similar to tarot cards, just with the runes on those. And within a week or so, as I continued to sit with that and meditate on it, the idea of synth [SP] dice came up. The 24 runes are often put in 3 rows of 8, so it's like an 8-sided dice, 1 for each row of the runes.

When you tap into that notion of story, as a writer, it just floods out and you're like, "Where did this come from?" I've workshopped it at Pikes Peak Writers Conference last weekend. I have the authors do their own layout and then I help them interpret what it means not knowing necessarily what their stories are, just giving the interpretation of what I'm seeing in the cards or the dice, and they're like, "That really applies. That works." That's kind of the genesis of it.

I've got four basic layouts that I use. One is just a really quick character sketch, which I've kind of based on Michael Hague's work. I have a couple that are good for scene work or for sequences in the story. And then, the larger layout that I have right now, it goes back to Campbell, to Story Grid, to John Truby's work... you can create an outline of your entire story with the crossing the thresholds, and the point-of-no-return, and the dark knight of the soul. That kind of stuff is in there along with the portions of antagonism and the helpers and allies and all that fun stuff.

It's been interesting to put this together. I'm working on an expanded layout that'll do the cards.

J.: The runes and the process you're developing is in order to get to an outline?

Marc: Essentially. Some of the people I've worked with are in the middle of a story. You can use it as a writing prompt. If you've gotten stuck and you've written yourself into a corner or just aren't sure where a scene is going, do a quick layout.

The book that I'm working on will be *Runes for Writers: Boost your Creativity and Destroy Writer's Block*. The intent is that you develop the tool. There's nothing magical about the runes. For me, it's a way to distract the left brain, which is where writer's block comes from, distract the left brain, get it thinking about some other problem. Then, the right brain is free to dive down into the unconscious to pull that story through.

I think the next big step is using it as an outline, to get the story more or less fleshed out. But it can definitely be a prompt, something to shake loose the creativity or create a daily writing practice. I think it can be used in a variety of ways. I'm still exploring all of those.

J.: How would you say runes is either alike or different from the way writers use tarot in storytelling?

Marc: The underlying principle is the same. The subconscious is influencing the shuffle. It's stacking the deck. It's putting the things in order so that your inner self, the muse, higher sources, whatever—the subconscious is so dialed in to story, to underlying currents of creativity, that you are unconsciously stacking the deck to for an answer. We need to get our ordinary consciousness out of the way. So, in that regard, I think they work very similarly.

For me, the runes are more effective. It's a symbol, a letter essentially, whereas the tarot have more developed scenes and visual representations. For me, the runes are more effective in that I'm not just looking at a scene and getting a prompt from that. The left brain is engaged in trying to characterize and quantify what I'm seeing on this card, what it means, and it's precisely that distraction that then allows the right brain to engage and dive into that subconscious communication.

J.: What are you hoping writers will be able to do with this? Once you have the book and the process in place, what's your grand dream or your aspirations for runes?

Marc: I'm a big believer in the power of story, the power of myth, and I think storytellers are the shamans of today. We look around the world. We see all the political troubles we have, social conflicts, everything. I believe that it's because we've lost our connection to myth. Myth is really the way that we tell our story to ourselves. And so, storytellers have power if they tap into it.

Writing for entertainment is great. People need to be distracted and to have a chance to escape into a different world. But there's also a real power in that. We've got the opportunity to provide subliminal healing and transformation for people, for our readers. There's a real opportunity to tell true, transformative stories and to kick-start our own methodology again. I'm really passionate about that aspect.

It's a great tool for expediency, for getting unstuck, for getting out of your own way and allowing the story to come through. But I think the more writers use tools like these and the more they develop that connection to the unconscious, what I call the source of story, that realm of creativity, the more they make that connection, and the easier that connection comes. They're rewiring the brain, creating new synaptic pathways, and becoming better conduits for the muse. It facilitates that process so much better and I think will open the gates to more powerful, easier, and more effective storytelling overall.

But I don't want runes to become dogmatic. My interpretation of the runes is somewhat different than some of the experts that are out there. The runes are the runes. It's like anything else. They represent a form of energy and you can either work against that flow, or you can go with it. But, the meaning is what the writer gives to it, what the reader gives to it. While I have a set interpretation that works for me, I do want people to know that as you work with them and become more familiar with them, they will tell you what they mean to you. The user's subconscious is stacking the deck and it's there to give them a specific message. Whether I would interpret it that way or not, the runes becomes their own, it will speak to them in their own way.

(Ed. Note: *Runes for Writers* was released by Erulian Press, 2019).

USING 12 OFFICIALS WITH JAMES R. ESSIEN

James is a good friend of mine and has been doing fascinating work using the ancient Chinese guide of the 12 Officials. He contributed this introductory piece for Three Story Method.

Uncle Bill's 12 Officials
An Ancient Chinese Guide to Story, Business, and Life

The Huangdi Neijing is an ancient medical text said to have been written by the mythical Yellow Emperor over 2,000 years ago. It laid the groundwork for Chinese Medicine, and is to this day one of its most important source works. Central to the ancient paradigm are the 12 energetic functions of the human body, each of which is named after an anatomical organ in the torso. To classical Chinese medical thinking, the function of the major organs was much broader than the biomedical functions we understand today. Rather, each organ was a manifestation of a larger energetic function.

· · ·

IN THE EIGHTH chapter of the text, the twelve organs and their specialized functions are described. The organs are referred to as 'officials' because their function within the body was said to be analogous to the function, dynamic, and hierarchy of officials within an imperial court. Chinese medicine practitioners spend many years studying each organ's elemental affinity, yin/yang quality, meridian pathways, etc., before coming to a full understanding.

THE ECCENTRIC AND irreverent Uncle Bill spent 30 years doing just that. In time, he began to notice that the dynamics at play within the human body—and that the Nei Jing describes being mirrored within an imperial court—also manifest within everyday group dynamics. From governments, corporate boardrooms, and classrooms, to the *Iliad*, *Star Trek*, and *Sons of Anarchy*, the natural structure of the 12 officials is present.

ORGAN FUNCTIONS and Group Dynamics

UNCLE BILL'S 12 Officials is an analogy between the functions of the human body and a group enterprise. It is a method of describing the *specialized functions* that emerge within a healthy group enterprise. Conversely, it is also a method for diagnosing the resulting pathology when a specialized function is absent, dominating, or otherwise dysfunctional. Understanding these dynamics and making them present within the relationships between your characters will make those relationships feel real.

· · ·

THE FOLLOWING IS a list of the 12 Officials and their corresponding function:3

Organ	Official
Heart	Lord and Master
Lung	Prime Minister
Liver	General
Gall Bladder	Champion
Pericardium	Envoy/Heart Protector
Spleen	Servant
Stomach	Cook
Small Intestine	Fool
Large Intestine	Asshole
Kidney	Technical Expert
Triple Warmer	Priest
Urinary Bladder	Provincial Governor

The 12 officials emerge naturally, like water droplets congealing into a hexagonal pattern. Six solid points (yang), and six voids (yin). And like a snowflake, the conditions have to be right for this to occur. Get a group of five people together just aimlessly hanging out, and the 12 officials will not necessarily appear. But when those five people make a concerted effort to achieve something—like cook an extravagant meal, go on an adventure, or plan a heist—then a dynamic will emerge that always takes a similar shape. Not only will a dynamic appear, but the character and success of the enterprise will depend on the functioning of all 12 officials.

THIS IS important for fiction writers, because *readers intuitively recognize the natural dynamic of the 12 roles.*

. . .

12 PEOPLE ARE NOT REQUIRED for a functional group, obviously. Two people can run a business... as long as all 12 roles are present between the two of them. In this hypothetical lean business, the two entrepreneurs will need:

HEART - LORD AND MASTER. A person or meaningful principle that exemplifies their ideals. When the Heart is a person, which it usually is, that person is not present. Rather, it is the spirit of the person—what they represent— which inspires the two entrepreneurs. Think Steve Jobs for media-tech start-ups. A mentor, either deceased or otherwise absent, often fills this role.

LUNG - THE ROLE of Prime Minister. This person makes large executive decisions, and inspires the other officials with their loyalty to the Heart.

LIVER - THE ROLE OF GENERAL. Someone needs to be the right-hand of the Lung. The Liver is responsible for strategy.

GALL BLADDER - THE CHAMPION. This role emerges as someone who rises up and takes the initiative to tackle a big problem, or spearheads the execution of a new tactic.

PERICARDIUM - THE ENVOY or Heart Protector. This is the face of the company. The Pericardium handles relations with the world outside the company. But it also has the closest connection to the Heart itself, and because of this, can remind the company of what it is working toward.

SPLEEN - SERVANT. There will be plenty of mundane tasks that need to be done unquestioningly.

STOMACH - THE COOK. Food is often overlooked, but an enterprise can live or die by its stomach.

LARGE INTESTINE - THE ASSHOLE. Nobody wants to be the Asshole, and that's the point. There will be tasks that need to be done that are unpleasant and unpopular. From firing vendors to confronting a partner about the elephant in the room, the garbage will need to be taken out occasionally.

SMALL INTESTINE - The office can get too cold without the Fool, who can make light of sensitive topics. Truth is easier to take when you're laughing, and stupid questions are often the most important.

KIDNEY - THE TECHNICAL EXPERT. Just like it sounds, this is the role of the engineer.

TRIPLE WARMER - THE PRIEST. From time to time, harmony will need to be restored to the officials. The priest can intervene to reconnect individuals to the greater purpose.

· · ·

URINARY BLADDER - This can be seen as the Sergeant. More broadly, the Urinary Bladder collects resources. For a successful enterprise, people will need to show up to work on time, do their jobs, and stop lollygagging when they should be working. Accounts receivable will need to be chased down. The Urinary Bladder becomes especially necessary when low-level employees are hired and need to be managed.

ALL 12 ROLES can be accomplished by the two-person start-up, and the roles can shift from person to person at different times. But if any of the roles are absent or dominating, then a pathology will result.

WHAT DOES a business start-up have to do with fiction? The above example may seem particular to a new company, but it's not. This happens to be what the 12 officials look like when they emerge in such a scenario, but the essential roles are the same no matter the enterprise.

READERS WILL FEEL that a group of characters that are on a mission will seem 'whole' when each official is being performed, no matter the number of characters. There is a sense that the group has become greater than the sum of its parts.

TAKE, for instance, the Fellowship of the Ring. Each of the nine members of the Fellowship clearly embody at least one official, and some do double-duty.

. . .

HEART (LORD and Master) - The triumph of good over evil, embodied by the once and future true king.

Lung (Prime Minister) - Aragorn

Liver (General) - Legolas

Gall Bladder (Champion) - Gimli

Pericardium (Envoy/Heart Protector) - Frodo

Spleen (Servant) - Samwise

Stomach (Cook) - Samwise

Large Intestine (Asshole) - Boromir

Small Intestine (Fool) - Pippin and Merry

Kidney (Technical Expert) - Gandalf

Triple Warmer (Priest) - Gandalf

Urinary Bladder (Sergeant) - Aragorn

NOTICE how these roles only emerged when the Fellowship was together on the mission. Before the Fellowship formed, and after it was broken up, the dynamics between characters was different.

ALTERNATIVELY, many (if not most) great stories are driven by a group pathology. For example, the crew in *The Life Aquatic with Steve Zissou*. This story features a nihilistic Lung/Prime Minister (Steve Zissou), an incompetent

Liver/General (Klaus), abused Spleens/Servants (the interns), and a disengaged and bitter Triple Warmer/Priest (Eleanor Zissou). These pathologies drive the comedy. However, it is interesting to note that the pathologies disappear during the climax when Steve Zissou finally channels the Heart (Esteban, represented by the Leopard Shark) as the Lung is supposed to. At that moment, the other officials fall into harmony.

THE FOLLOWING IS a list of well-known characters from books, movies, and TV shows that epitomize their respective official:

Organ	Official	Fictional Example
Heart	Lord and Master	John Teller (*Sons of Anarchy*)
Lung	Prime Minister	Malcolm Reynolds (*Firefly*)
Liver	General	Davos Seaworth (*Game of Thrones*)
Gall Bladder	Champion	Achilles (*The Iliad*)
Pericardium	Envoy/Heart Protector	Ned (*The Life Aquatic*)
Spleen	Servant	Alfred Pennyworth (*Batman*)
Stomach	Cook	Mrs. Weasley (*Harry Potter*)
Small Intestine	Fool	Pippin (*Lord of the Rings*)
Large Intestine	Asshole	Douglas (*Bird Box*, the movie)
Kidney	Technical Expert	Scotty (*Star Trek*)
Triple Warmer	Priest	The Oracle (*The Matrix*)
Urinary Bladder	Provincial Governor	Sergeant Hartman (*Full Metal Jacket*)

THERE ARE countless fascinating archetypes in fiction. The 12 officials are not archetypes, per se. Rather, they are specialized functions that naturally arise. Any archetypal character can find themselves filling any of the roles.

. . .

HAVING SAID THAT, the roles themselves are named after familiar archetypes. For example, the Small Intestine is a specialized function. It is a yang organ. Its element is fire, and it is paired with the Heart. The Nei Jing says its function is to 'separate the clear from the turbid.' Uncle Bill says that the specialized function manifests in groups as the 'Fool.'

THE FOOL IS a familiar archetype in the West. Many kings employed a court jester to make light of issues that nobody else would dare to. Jesters would often get away with insulting noblemen who were present in the room, and sometimes even the king himself. A wise king knows how crucial this role is for the health of the court.

THE FOOL (SMALL INTESTINE), has a special connection to the Lord and Master (Heart). The Heart is yin-fire, and the Small Intestine is yang-fire. Wisdom and insight are often channeled through the comedian. As the Fool can get members of the enterprise to drop their guard, wisdom and insight are better able to penetrate. A group pathology of the Small Intestine would present as the Fool being ignored, persecuted, or absent altogether.

WE'VE ONLY SCRATCHED the surface. Learning about each official's element (fire, metal, wood, earth, water), yin/yang affinity, and relationship to other officials, will make clear what most readers already intuitively grasp. An understanding of Uncle Bill's 12 Officials will give you the ability to deliberately create either a strong group of characters that is greater than the sum of its parts, or a richly pathological group that blusters through a scene with its own idiosyncratic limp.

MIND MAPPING WITH CHRISTOPHER WILLS

Christopher and I have been friends for many years, and he's a certified Mind Mapping instructor. He contributed this introductory piece for *Three Story Method*.

MIND MAPPING **by Christopher Wills**

A lot of writers use mind maps or similar diagrams as a tool in their writing career. In this section, I will answer some frequently asked questions about mind maps:

What is a mind map and how does one draw a mind map?
What are the advantages of mind mapping to an author?
What parts of the author business can mind mapping be used for?
How can I mind map if I am not artistic and can't draw?
Can I mind map digitally?
What are the best uses of mind mapping for an author?

WHAT IS a mind map and how does one draw a mind map?

A MIND MAP IS A POWERFUL, colorful and graphic tool that will increase your creativity, improve your learning and understanding, and speed up your thinking by accessing parts of your brain you don't normally use for these tasks.

TO DRAW A SIMPLE MIND MAP:

1. Choose a title or working title and write it in the center of a piece of plain paper, landscape orientation. If you are able (or brave), try and create an image or doodle as part of the title. For example, if the mind map is the brainstorming part of your novel, why not draw a simple doodle of the book as the image and write the title in the center of your book. Why not color this title in?
2. Choose the important initial ideas (subtitles) and create a branch for each radiating out from the central title. Write the name, preferably one word only, on each branch – so your mind map might now look like a starfish.
3. Create second level ideas (sub-subtitles), each of which branch out from relevant subtitles like twigs on a tree.
4. Write one word on each twig.
5. If required, create third-level ideas out from the twigs, writing one word on each.

6. Wherever possible, add images, sketches, or doodles that are representative of the idea.
7. Use color to link ideas, for example, everything along a subtitle in one color, or draw a cloud behind linked ideas and color in the cloud.
8. Add links between branches or twigs if the ideas are linked.

PRESTO, you have drawn a mind map. It might be a mess. It might be lopsided with most of the data on one half of the page. You might look at it and think of more ideas you want to add. Armed with the finished product why not redraw it, balancing out the data and using color to link data and add your extra data.

NOW YOU MIGHT HAVE something to be proud of. Something to put on your wall or magnet onto your magnetic whiteboard.

DID it get your brain thinking? Does the finished product inspire you? Are you proud of it? You should be.

THREE FEATURES differentiate good mind mapping from traditional linear notes:

1. **A central title image.** The title is placed in the center of a page and is normally part of a

representative image in the form of a simple doodle rather than an artistic drawing.

2. **Radiating branches**. The main subtitles radiate out from the central image like starfish legs, each having one word to denote the subtitle. Each leg should be a different color to further differentiate each subtitle. These legs have sub-legs radiating from their ends like smaller branches on a tree, each also using one word for the sub-subtitle, and if appropriate maintaining the color scheme.

3. **Color, pictures (simple doodle images are common), patterns, codes, and symbols** are added to further enhance the colorful, visual, radial and non-linear shape of the mind map.

WHAT ARE **the advantages of mind mapping to an author?**

CHEAP. I prefer to hand-draw my mind maps. This means I don't need expensive hardware or software to use mind mapping as a tool. Also, it means I can be very portable with my mind mapping. A good portable starter kit might be an A5 unlined notebook and a cheap set of colored pens. Even cheaper, but don't tell anyone, go to your kid's bedroom and "borrow" the paper and colored pens or pencils from under their bed or deep in the back of their wardrobe – they will never notice.

ONE ADVANTAGE of hand drawing mind maps is no matter where you are in your travels it is easy to find a cheap note-book or pad and colored pens in corner shops, stationery stores, or supermarkets.

IT IS AN EASILY PORTABLE TOOL. We will return to software, honest, but ignoring it for the moment, a typical kit I own is an A4 art pad, a set of colored pens and a cheap plastic document wallet to carry them in. This can easily be slipped into a backpack to be available when needed. A simpler kit for walkabout without a backpack would be one of the many A5 notebooks, now available, with unlined pages, and a couple of pens or pencils. I find 3 colors are plenty for producing acceptable first-draft mind maps or for idea creation when sitting in a park, on a train, in a café, etc.

MIND MAPPING WILL STIMULATE **your creativity.** If you are

starting a new project, or are stuck for ideas, or have written yourself into a blind alley, drawing a mind map is a great way to access your creative right brain. Writing traditional linear notes does not need your creative right brain so it can limit your thinking. Because mind mapping uses colors, images, shapes, radiant design, etc., it needs access to the right side of your brain and research has shown this will improve your ability to think creatively.

WHAT PARTS of the author business can mind mapping be used for?

MIND MAPPING CAN BE USED for anything an author might write on paper; it is simply a different way, a more advanced and advantageous way, of taking and recording notes. Mind mapping can be used by authors in 3 different areas:

- Creativity
- Business, management & marketing
- Life

CREATIVITY - FICTION

IN FICTION, one can use mind mapping as a creative tool to generate and organize ideas from a blank page and a blank mind. Typically this might be a brainstorming session to create a story, or to dream up some characters, or to decide on settings, or to solve a problem such as, "How do I get my character out of the mess I wrote her into?"

ONE OF THE many uses in fiction might be to outline a story. One should choose one's favorite outline structure and knowledge of the tropes of the genre, to create a boilerplate mind map. This could be saved on a computer and reused if one was writing a series or more books in the genre. One could print a copy of the boilerplate mind map and use it in two different ways:

- As a stimulant to nudge one as to the requirements for the story outline;
- As a starting-point guide to draw an original mind map outline of your story.

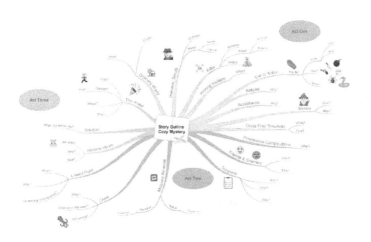

A BOILERPLATE MIND map for cozy mystery drawn using iMindMap11 software.

I CREATED this boilerplate based on the Hero's Journey. It may not be your structure of choice. That's okay. Create your own boilerplate mind map to suit your own needs. As I suggested, I could print this and pin it to the wall next to my whiteboard to prompt me of the things I need to consider when creating my outline. Or I could redraw this replacing the prompt words with ideas at the appropriate points.

YES, I could create a prompt sheet, such as a linear form to fill in. But that would not access the right side of my brain and thus, may not produce as much creative thinking and such a good story outline.

SOMETHING TO NOTE IS that any part of a mind map can (and should) be used as the starting point for a further deeper mind map. In this case, for example, you might choose to further develop the killer. So new blank sheet, killer doodle at center then radiate ideas out such as childhood, parents, career problems, hobbies, dark secret, etc., whatever you need.

CREATIVITY - NONFICTION

A MIND MAP can be used in a brainstorming way to generate every part of a non-fiction book:

- the initial idea for the book
- the question the book answers
- the title
- the structure of the book – its contents
- the chapter titles
- the content and structure of each chapter
- images and symbols for the cover.

Business, management, and marketing

Mind maps can be used to help in anything a writer might want to create, record, write, plan or solve, e.g.:

1. SWOT analysis
2. BCG Product analysis
3. Planning
4. Product, Place or Price analysis
5. A marketing mix brainstorm
6. Problem-solving
7. Etc.

This list is only limited by one's imagination, but let's consider a couple on the list.

SWOT analysis

- Draw a symbol to represent the book or genre or

series or your publishing company at the center of a blank page.

- Add four main branches labeling them Strengths, Weaknesses, Opportunities, and Threats.
- Brainstorm off each branch and note how sometimes a Strength is also a Weakness and an Opportunity is also a Threat – you may not notice this if you use linear notes.

Planning

- Write "week," "month" or your chosen planning period at the center of a blank page.
- Draw radiating branches from the center to represent time divisions (e.g., if it is a weekly plan, you will need five, six, or seven branches, one for each working day).
- On the end of each branch, radiate smaller branches or twigs, depending on what you plan to attack for that day. This non-linear style can represent a refreshing way to look at the working week.

Marketing Mix Brainstorm

One way to do this would be to create a boilerplate with Marketing as the central title and a branch to represent each of the ways one can market a book (e.g., Amazon Ads, FB Ads, Website posts, Newsletter swaps, Email list pushes, Twitter, Instagram, Local radio, Local Press, etc.).

THIS BOILERPLATE WOULD NEED to be initially brainstormed to ensure every viable way you might consider to market a book was represented by a branch, then each branch would be the focus of a brainstorm about cost, viability, ease of use, potential return, etc.

AS A SECOND STEP, each branch could become the central title to create a new mind map on just that type of marketing, with the main advantages and disadvantages transferred back to the original mind map for comparison.

Problem-solving

Correct mind mapping using the Laws says that one should only use one word per branch, and in problem-solving, this can be very important.

WHY?

Consider the problem of a book launch that didn't work. I know nobody has ever had one of these but bear with... One could call this problem "Sci-Fi Book Launch."

USING TRADITIONAL PROBLEM-SOLVING TECHNIQUES, or using that as the title of a branch on a mind map could lead one along the wrong path to a solution.

. . .

How come?

Consider this. A blank piece of paper. Central title is the name of the book, and an image could be the book cover. If we had only one branch labeled "Sci-Fi Book Launch," what might our analysis come up with?

1. Timing - maybe other better books were launched at the same time, or maybe it was not a good time to launch a new book, or maybe we should have waited until we had two more books then rapid released, etc.
2. Marketing – maybe we should have used Amazon instead of FB, or both, or spent more money, or designed better ads, or used an email list to create ARCs, etc.
3. And so on.

What are we doing? Because we are concentrating on the whole phrase "Sci-Fi Book Launch" we believe it is only one topic, probably the "launch," so that is the problem we are trying to solve.

But what if we had three branches on our mind map, one labeled "Sci-Fi," one labeled "Book" and one labeled "Launch"?

. . .

NOW WE ARE FORCIBLY DRAWING our attention to the fact that there are three parts to our problem. So let's consider the word "Sci-Fi":

- Was this the right genre for our book?
- Were there other major writers launching in this genre on the same day or week?
- Do our target readers expect to find our books under Sci-Fi or would a narrower genre descriptor make it easier for them, like Military Sci-Fi, Post Apoc, Space Opera Sci-Fi, etc.?

NOW LET'S CONSIDER "BOOK":

- Is the cover good enough?
- Is the blurb good enough?
- Have we had a good-enough edit?
- Do we have the right number of words for this genre?
- Have we met the tropes for this genre? (Do we meet our target readers' expectations?).

YOU CAN SEE that by separating the three words in "Sci-Fi Book Launch" on a mind map, we are helping our mind to think outside of the limits, the traditional linear problem title of "Sci-Fi Book Launch" has channeled us toward.

LIFE

Unfortunately, most authors need to live in normal society, but no problem because mind mapping can help us. One can use mind mapping for:

- Planning daily, weekly, monthly and annual routines
- Shopping lists – create a boilerplate mind map using items one buys every week and leave space for add-ons, e.g., for special meals. One could create say, a BBQ template with everything one needs for a BBQ with only quantities needing to be added. One could even arrange each branch to be equivalent to an aisle in the supermarket. Believe it or not, if you did this, you would eventually not need the mind map shopping list because the mind map format will have helped you to memorize everything on the shopping list.

How can I mind map if I am not artistic and can't draw?

No such thing as not artistic. If an unmade bed, a pile of bricks, a monument wrapped in tissue paper and an empty white room with a flickering neon light is art, what does not artistic mean?

Sorry about that, but I had to say it. The truth is, one does not need to be artistic as mind mapping is more like doodling than art.

. . .

FOR EXAMPLE, if one wants to draw a man, draw a stick figure, a woman, replace the stick body with a triangle and maybe add some hair to the stick head. If one wants to represent emotions like happiness, sadness, etc., draw simple emoticons. If one wants to represent a house, draw a square with a triangle on top for the roof; a hospital, draw a rectangle with a cross in a circle near the top; a car, draw two wheels and a couple of rectangles on top.

THIS IS NOT ART, it is representing something using an image. If your 5 year old draws a picture of Mummy and Daddy holding hands in front of your house, you can instantly see what they have drawn without thinking you have a future Leonardo da Vinci or Edward Hopper in the family.

CAN I MIND MAP DIGITALLY?

THERE ARE many mind-mapping software packages of varying qualities available, some free and others ranging from cheap to less cheap, but none yet are that expensive. Google (or another search engine) "free mind map software" as a start. Add "top ten," and you will find a lot of examples.

BUT BEFORE YOU get out your wallet or purse, I suggest you look at your current computer to see if you already have a mind-mapping tool. For example, *Visio* is part of the Microsoft Office package (or it's an add-on). It's very basic but if it's already on your PC, have a play with it before you look for something to buy. It will help you learn a little about the potential of software mind mapping. Also, try some of the free mind mapping tools before you think of spending money.

THE FIRST THING TO say is that some of the so-called mind mapping software is not mind mapping because it doesn't allow one to use color, symbols, images, codes, and patterns. I would call these tools scatter diagram tools rather than mind mapping tools. Nothing wrong with them but to engage the right side of the brain and put one into the fully creative mode, I suggest one needs a tool that easily allows one to use color, symbols, images, codes, and patterns.

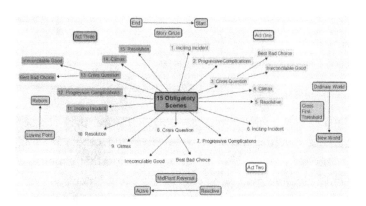

PERSONALLY, I would encourage you to hand-draw your mind maps before you experiment with software because hand-drawn mind maps:

- Are simple to create something – you only need paper and crayons
- Are quick to create something
- Able to be drawn anywhere without having to carry electronics. And if you don't have a pad of paper and colored pens, almost every newsagent in the world sells them.
- Do not have the barrier of having to learn how to use a piece of software.
- Engage the brain more than pressing keys or moving a mouse, etc. Therefore, you will be more creative by hand-drawing a mind map.

IMPORTANT POINT - **the power of the mind map is in the creation, not in the finished product.**

LOOK at the three examples I have shown in this chapter. Some may look at the iMindMap 11 example and say that is the best-looking mind map. But it doesn't matter what the finished product looks like. The power of the mind map is the creative thinking one does while creating it. You are trying to solve a problem or imagine a new story, not create a pretty picture.

IF YOU PRACTICE DRAWING mind maps, you will get better (a bit like writing...). You will soon be able to quickly and easily produce colorful, creative mind maps that will look good on your walls, that you can be proud of, that others will admire.

. . .

A SCENARIO where some prefer software is when giving a presentation because some software helps users to create presentations, but again, one needs to learn how to use it. Personally, I draw my title, scan it into the computer. Add the first branch to the image, scan that in, etc., adding each image in sequence to presentation slides.

WHAT ARE the best uses of mind mapping for an author?

MIND MAPPING IS at its best when used for anything creative where one needs to brainstorm for ideas. For example, at the start where one is brainstorming ideas about the story, characters, setting, and themes, etc. Also, when writing where one has written oneself into a blind alley, and one desperately wants to get out of it, or if one has run out of ideas. Typically, this might happen when writing the dreaded Act Two. Try mind mapping for just Act Two to stimulate new ideas.

THIS WAS ONLY a quick summary of the many ways that mind mapping can be useful to an author.

MIND MAPPING CAN BE USED on many levels for many projects. Even if you don't use it in researching and preparing to write a novel, you can gain benefits in so many other ways.

WORKS CITED

Ackerman, Angela, and Becca Puglisi. *The Negative Trait Thesaurus: A Writer's Guide to Character Flaws*. JADD Publishing, 2013.

"Ancient Aliens: Collector's Edition." *Ancient Aliens*.

Aristotle, and James Hutton. *Aristotle's Poetics*. Penguin Books, 1996.

Atwood, Margaret. "MasterClass Online Classes." *MasterClass*, www.masterclass.com/.

Baldacci, David. "MasterClass Online Classes." *MasterClass*, www.masterclass.com/.

Bell, James Scott. *The Art of War for Writers: Fiction Writing Strategies, Tactics, and Exercises*. Writer's Digest Books, 2011.

Blume, Judy. "MasterClass Online Classes." *MasterClass*, www.masterclass.com/.

Brody, Jessica. *Save the Cat! Writes a Novel*. Ten Speed Press, 2018.

Brown, Dan. "MasterClass Online Classes." *MasterClass*, www.masterclass.com/.

Campbell, Joseph. *The Hero with a Thousand Faces*. New World Library, 2008.

Campbell, Joseph, and Bill D. Moyers. *Joseph Campbell and the Power of Myth with Bill Moyers*. Kino Lorber, 2018.

Clear, James. *Atomic Habits: Tiny Changes, Remarkable Results: An Easy & Proven Way to Build Good Habits & Break Bad Ones*. Avery, an Imprint of Penguin Random House, 2018.

Cleaver, Jerry. *Immediate Fiction: A Complete Writing Course*. St. Martin's Press, 2002.

Coyne, Shawn. *The Story Grid: What Good Editors Know*. Black Irish Entertainment, 2015.

Daigle, Christine. "The Impact of the New Translation of the Second Sex: Rediscovering Beauvoir." *Journal of Speculative Philosophy*, Vol. 27, No. 3, (2013), pp. 336-347.

Donahue, Caroline. *Story Arcana: Tarot for Writers*. Secret Library Press, 2019.

Fox, Chris. *Write to Market: Deliver a Book that Sells*. 2016.

Gaiman, Neil. "MasterClass Online Classes." *MasterClass*, www.masterclass.com/.

Gladwell, Malcolm. "MasterClass Online Classes." *MasterClass*, www.masterclass.com/.

Godin, Seth. "Akimbo." Stitcher.com (podcast), 2020. http://www.stitcher.com/podcast/pods/akimbo.

Graham, Marc. *Runes for Writers: Boost Your Creativity and Destroy Writer's Block (Shaman of Story)*. Erulian Press, 2019.

Hawker, Libbie. *Take off Your Pants!: Outline Your Books for Faster, Better Writing*. Running Rabbit Press, 2015.

Homer, and Robert Fitzgerald. *The Odyssey*. Vintage Books, 1990.

Hudson, Kim. *The Virgin's Promise: Writing Stories of Feminine Creative, Spiritual, and Sexual Awakening*. Michael Wiese Productions, 2011.

Kenrick, Douglas T., et al. "Renovating the Pyramid of Needs: Contemporary Extensions Built Upon Ancient Foundations." *Perspectives on Psychological Science: A Journal of the Association for Psychological Science*, U.S. National Library of Medicine, May 2010, www.ncbi.nlm.nih.gov/pmc/articles/PMC3161123/.

Kaire, Steve. "5 High Concept Requirements Defined Once and For All." http://www.writersstore.com/high-concept-defined-once-and-for-all/.

Kenrick, Douglas T., et al. "Renovating the Pyramid of Needs: Contemporary Extensions Built Upon Ancient Foundations." *Perspectives on Psychological Science: A Journal of the Association for Psychological Science*, U.S. National Library of Medicine, May 2010, www.ncbi.nlm.nih.gov/pmc/articles/PMC3161123/.

King, Stephen. *On Writing: A Memoir Of the Craft*. Pocket Books, 2000.

Leonelle, Monica. *The 8-Minute Writing Habit: Create a Consistent Writing Habit That Works With Your Busy Lifestyle*. Spaulding House, 2015.

"Learning to Be Present With Yourself." *Psychology Today*,

Sussex Publishers, www.psychologytoday.com/ca/blog/the-mindful-self-express/201204/learning-be-present-yourself? collection=107816.

Mahin, Mark. "Nature Seems to Love the Number Three." *Future and Cosmos*, 1 Jan. 1970, http://futureandcosmos. blogspot.com/2014/01/nature-seems-to-love-number-three.html.

Mamet, David. "MasterClass Online Classes." *MasterClass*, www.masterclass.com/.

Maslow, Abraham. "A Theory of Human Motivation." *Psychological Review*, 1949.

McDonald, Brian. *Invisible Ink: a Practical Guide to Building Stories That Resonate*. Talking Drum, 2017.

McDonald, Brian. *The Golden Theme: How to Make Your Writing Appeal to the Highest Common Denominator*. Talking Drum, LLC, 2017.

McKee, Robert. *Story: Substance, Structure, Style, and the Principles of Screenwriting*. HarperCollins, 2010.

Murdock, Maureen. *The Heroine's Journey*. Shambhala, 1990.

Oates, Joyce Carol. "MasterClass Online Classes." *Master-Class*, www.masterclass.com/.

Patterson, James. "MasterClass Online Classes." *MasterClass*, www.masterclass.com/.

Pink, Daniel H. *To Sell Is Human: The Surprising Truth about Persuading, Convincing, and Influencing Others*. Canongate Books LTD, 2018.

Pressfield, Steven. *The War of Art: Break through the Blocks and Win Your Inner Creative Battles*. Black Irish Entertainment, 2012.

Price, Brian. *Classical Storytelling and Contemporary Screenwriting: Aristotle and the Modern Scriptwriter*. Routledge, 2017.

Rhimes, Shonda. "MasterClass Online Classes." *MasterClass*, www.masterclass.com/.

Shmoop Editorial Team. "Star Wars: A New Hope: Hero's Journey." *Shmoop*, Shmoop University, 11 Nov. 2008, www.shmoop.com/star-wars-a-new-hope/heros-journey.html.

Snyder, Blake. *Save the Cat!: the Last Book on Screenwriting You'll Ever Need*. Michael Wiese Productions, 2005.

Sorkin, Aaron. "MasterClass Online Classes." *MasterClass*, www.masterclass.com/.

Stine, R. L. "MasterClass Online Classes." *MasterClass*, www.masterclass.com/.

Stone, Todd. *Novelist's Boot Camp: 101 Ways to Take Your Book from Boring to Bestseller*. Writer's Digest Books, 2006.

"The Tarot and the Hero's Journey." *The Tarot Channel*, 21 Mar. 2017, thetarotchannel.com/the-heros-journey/.

"This Is Akimbo." *This Is Akimbo*, Season 3, Episode 8, www.akimbo.me/.

Three, Rule of. "What Is the Mysterious 'Rule of Three'?" *Rule of Three Copywriting Studio*, http://rule-of-three.co.uk/what-is-the-rule-of-three-copywriting.

Vogler, Christopher. *The Writer's Journey: Mythic Structure for Writers*. Michael Wiese Productions, 2007.

Weiland, K. M. *Creating Character Arcs: the Masterful Author's Guide to Uniting Story Structure, Plot, and Character Development*. PenForASword, 2016.

Williamson, Jill. *Storyworld First: Creating a Unique Fantasy World for Your Novel*. Novel Teen Press, 2014.

Wright, Will. "MasterClass Online Classes." *MasterClass*, www.masterclass.com/.

ABOUT J. THORN

J. Thorn is a Top 100 Most Popular Author in Horror, Science Fiction, Action & Adventure and Fantasy (Amazon Author Rank). He has published two million words and has sold more than 185,000 books worldwide. In March of 2014 Thorn held the #5 position in Horror alongside his childhood idols Dean Koontz and Stephen King (at #4 and #2 respectively). He is an official member of the Science Fiction and Fantasy Writers of America, the Horror Writers Association, and the Great Lakes Association of Horror Writers.

Thorn earned a B.A. in American History from the University of Pittsburgh and a M.A. from Duquesne University. He is a full-time writer, part-time professor at John Carroll University, co-owner of Molten Universe Media, podcaster, FM radio DJ, musician, and a certified Story Grid nerd.

https://theauthorlife.com

ABOUT ZACH BOHANNON

 Zach Bohannon is a science fiction, horror, and dark fantasy author. His critically acclaimed post-apocalyptic zombie series, Empty Bodies, is a former Amazon #1 bestseller. Along with J. Thorn, he hosts The Career Author, a weekly podcast helping writers achieve their dreams of turning their art into a full-time profession. They organize several unique experiences for authors, including The Career Author Summit and Authors on a Train. The pair also co-own Molten Universe Media, a publishing company specializing in post-apocalyptic fiction. He lives in Tennessee with his wife, daughter, and their German shepherd.

www.zachbohannon.com

CPSIA information can be obtained
at www.ICGtesting.com
Printed in the USA
LVHW041231111220
673919LV00004B/138

9 781393 009894